Tippu Tip

TIPPU TIP

The Story of His Career in Zanzibar & Central Africa

Narrated from his own accounts
By Dr Heinrich Brode

Translated from Arabic by H. Havelock

With a preface by Sir Charles Elliot

The Gallery Publications
Zanzibar 2000

Published in 2000 by:
The Gallery Publications
P.O. Box 3181, 170 Gizenga Street, Zanzibar
e mail: gallery@swahilicoast.com

(c) 2000 by The Gallery Publications for the corrected and modern translation

All rights reserved. No part of this publication may be reproduced or transmitted in any form or by any means, electronic or mechanical, including photographing, recording or any information storage and retrieval system, without written permission from the publishers

ISBN 9987 8877 6 7

Cover photo : Tippu Tip

Design: The Swahili Coast Publishers

CONTENTS

EDITORIAL NOTE

PREFACE

AUTHOR'S PREFACE

CHAPTER I - Page 1
HISTORICAL INTRODUCTION: EAST AFRICA UP TO THE REIGN OF SEYYID SAID (1806-1856)

CHAPTER II - Page 7
THE FIRST JOURNEYS OF TIPPU TIP

CHAPTER III - Page 13
JOURNEY TO ITAHUA

CHAPTER IV - Page 23
EXPERIENCES IN ZANZIBAR AND FRESH JOURNEY TO CENTRAL AFRICA

CHAPTER V - Page 29
FROM UGALLA TO THE KINGDOM OF LUNDA

CHAPTER VI - Page 35
ENTRY TO URUA

CHAPTER VII - Page 41
THE NEW SULTAN OF UTETERA

CHAPTER VIII - Page 49
THE ARAB TOWNS OF NYANGWE AND KASSONGO

CHAPTER IX - Page 55
WITH STANLEY DOWN THE CONGO

CHAPTER X - Page 67
BY TABORA BACK TO ZANZIBAR

CHAPTER XI - Page 81
FRESH JOURNEY TO STANLEY FALLS

CHAPTER XII - Page 87
RETURN HOME

CHAPTER XIII - Page 95
THE FIGHTING ROUND STANLEY FALLS

CHAPTER XIV - Page 101
THE EMIN PASHA EXPEDITION

CHAPTER XV - Page 113
RETURN TO ZANZIBAR-COLLAPSE OF THE ARAB POWER
ON THE EAST AFRICA COAST

CHAPTER XVI - Page 125
THE COLLAPSE OF THE ARAB POWER

EDITORIAL NOTE

The editor of a book like this, which was translated into English nearly a century ago, faces a number of challenges. Some words, spellings and terms now seem archaic and outmoded. It seems fairly natural to change "thither" to "there" and "Tippoo Tib" to "Tippu Tip". It takes more judgement to change "Mohammedanism" to "Islam", "Negro" to "African" and "savage" to "native". It was trickier deciding what to do with comments which are racially offensive and, with some misgivings, I have left these in, rather than excise whole sentences from the text. I have also left untouched the word "heathen". It is perhaps worth noting that the slurs are restricted to Arabs, Africans and Indians - the Germans and the British get off scot-free.

Mark Wilson
July 2000.

Tippu Tip

PREFACE

The name of Tippu Tip is familiar to all who took an interest in he affairs of East Africa or the Congo fifteen or twenty years ago. He was the most remarkable of the band of Arab traders and explorers who, starting from the East Coast, penetrated to the Congo, and were the rulers of whatever country they happened to be in, though they established no states and did not even claim the right of conquest on behalf of their Sovereign, the Sultan of Zanzibar. It is curious to notice how much and how little they effected. They traversed enormous distances, and demonstrated the practicability of many routes through native kingdoms which were commonly considered pathless wildernesses; but they made no attempt to attach these regions to Zanzibar, or even to convert them to Islam.

The whole history of the Arabs in East Africa shows the same characteristics. They founded their cities on the coast, but made little effort to move inland, and in the rare cases where they did so, as at Tabora and Ujiji, the reason was simply that their slave-raids had depopulated the region near the sea, and they were forced to move on to districts where the game was not so shy. But their territorial and political instincts were feeble. The effective power of the Sultan rarely extended more then ten miles inland from the shore of the mainland. Beyond that limit, every Arab assumed the right to deal with the natives exactly as he pleased. But, however successful he might be, he did not extend the Sultan's authority, and if he perished, the Sultan did not feel called on to avenge his death.

Dr. Brode, who has had exceptional opportunities for studying the career of Tippu Tip, published some time ago in the 'Proceedings of the Institute of Oriental Languages' his autobiography, transcribed in Roman letters from his own manuscript, and accompanied by a translation. This work is now supplemented by a biography giving a connected chronological account of this adventurous career, which is worth reading both as a story and as a valuable addition to the obscure and scanty records of African history.

Its hero, Hamed bin Mohammed, better known by his nickname of Tippu Tip, was of mixed Arab and African descent, and the latter strain showed itself markedly in his physiognomy. Still, according to the ideas of Zanzibar, he was an Arab. Few dates are mentioned in his life until near the end. Arabs rarely know their ages exactly or keep any accurate diary. He was born in Zanzibar, and at the age of about eighteen went on a journey to Ujiji with his father, and continued it by himself to Urua, thus inaugurating the long series of trading expeditions which formed the occupation of his life. The chief objects of these expeditions were slaves and ivory. Ivory was plentiful, and the natives, who had often no notion of its value, were ready to sell it absurdly cheaply. If they made difficulties, vigorous measures were adopted without scruple or hesitation. The journey to Urua was succeeded by another to Urungu, at the southern end of Lake Tanganyika, in the course of which Tippu Tip met Livingstone near Lake Mueru.

These were comparatively short journeys, but Tippu Tip now proceeded to make a much more serious expedition, which was the foundation of his influence and importance. He seems to have started about 1867, and was away some fifteen years. Most of this time was spent in what is now the territory of the Congo Free State. There were Arab settlements in these regions, for the great distance from Zanzibar and the necessity of having some fortified centre and base of operations had obliged the traders to depart somewhat from their habits of predacious migration. We hear that their headquarters-Nyangwe-was a considerable town, with so many rice-fields round it that it was called New Bengal. His doings during this long absence are described in considerable detail. Part of the time he bore the title of Sultan of Utetera.

According to his own account, he claimed the sultanate in virtue of a perfectly fictitious relationship between his mother and the local royal family, with the result that the reigning Sultan resigned peacefully in his favour the day after he arrived. One cannot help suspecting that there is some slight lacuna in the narrative here. During this period he met Cameron, and also Stanley, whom he guided for a part of his journey towards the end of 1876. After parting from Stanley, he again spent some time in warring and trading, both in Kassongo and Tabora. He met Wissmann, and escorted him to the coast, and, as Dr. Brode says, if anything can justify his life it is that he was a faithful guide to Cameron, Stanley, and Wissmann, and had no small share in their success, though it must be admitted that his relations with these eminent explorers were not unruffled.

His relations with Stanley were renewed in 1887. After returning to Zanzibar in 1882, he went back to Utetera, but after a short absence was summoned home again by the Sultan. When Stanley organized his mission for the relief of Emin, he invited Tippu Tip to accompany him as guide, and, on behalf of the King of the Belgians, offered him the title of Governor of certain provinces of the Congo Free State. Details of this expedition, which was Tippu Tip's last important performance, are given in the biography.

It must be admitted that Tippu Tip was a slave-trader. These pages, based upon his own statements, give some inkling of the unscrupulous cruelty with which he dealt with natives, and clearly much remains untold, In excuse, one can only say that the cruelty of the slave-traders was no greater than the cruelty of the natives to one another. One eminent Arab, when criticized by Europeans for his slave-trading propensities, used to relate how he had fallen in with a tribe who were accustomed to eat their prisoners of war. He bought all these prisoners for a small sum, and made them his slaves, which he maintained, with a logic difficult to controvert, was far better for them than the other fate. Still, no doubt Tippu Tip's commercial journeys were in the main plundering expeditions. Anything else, any introduction of law and order, any spread of civilization, was merely subsidiary and incidental. But he was intelligent, not wantonly brutal, as many traders were; he had a far better idea of organizing a rough-and-ready administration than most Arabs, and he was always friendly to Europeans. By the assistance which he rendered to them he indirectly contributed in no small measure to the civilization of Africa, for which the Arabs themselves have done so little.

He was practically King of an enormous territory, but his power was never officially recognized even by his own Sovereign. Had it been, the future of East and Central Africa might have been materially changed, for the chief argument advanced by the European Powers who appropriated the hinterland behind the coast was that the Sultan had no effective jurisdiction over the natives there. But, as Dr. Brode points out, Seyyid Bargash, the Sultan of the period, had no talent or inclination for politics, and cared only for trade in its crudest aspect. He wished to get as much ivory as possible from the interior, but he did not care anything about the position and character of the countries which produced it. Yet perhaps pessimism rather than stupidity was the motive of his conduct. 'Hamed,' he said to Tippu Tip, 'be not angry with me; I want to have no more to do with the mainland. The Europeans want to take Zanzibar here from me; how should I be able to keep the mainland?' And Tippu Tip adds: 'When I heard those words I knew that it was all up with us.' It certainly was. The Sultan's dominions on the mainland soon became little more than a legal fiction, and he retains Zanzibar only on condition of also accepting the doubtful blessing of British protection.

The disappearance of the Arabs from East and Central Africa can hardly give cause for regret. They were seen at their best in such men as our hero, who, if he had had a free hand, might have established a firm if somewhat rapacious Government. But, on the whole, they were merely a nation of slave-traders, without much dignity or romance, and illustrated the demoralizing effect of slavery on the slave-owner. In the towns on the coast, where they had plantations, and in the island of Zanzibar, cultivation was kept up by a wasteful profusion of slave labour; but they were careless of the interior though they knew its good points and potentialities far better than Europeans. For administration, development, even for conquest, they showed complete apathy. They cared for nothing but the simple right to help themselves to valuables when and how they chose. They were destructive, and did not even preserve any good that they might find in native institutions. Had they retained any considerable tract of country, such beneficial legislation as the abolition of the slave-trade, and the prohibition to import alcohol and weapons within a certain zone, would probably have proved impossible.

I used to see Tippu Tip occasionally when I was His Majesty's Agent and Consul-General in Zanzibar in 1901 and 1902. His features were of the African type, and produced at first an impression that he was a low-caste hybrid; but this impression was dispelled by his polite and dignified manners and his flow of speech. The tremulous twitching of his eyelids was very noticeable, and it was generally believed that this was the origin of his name Tippu Tip, 'the blinker,' although he himself, not liking the personal allusion, had other explanations. The touch of mockery in his manner and language, to which Dr. Brode more than once alludes, was very noticeable, but not unpleasant nor discourteous. He did not live to execute the journey to Europe which Dr. Brode tells us he was planning, but, not long ago, in the language of Islam, he removed to 'the abode of permanency,' though some Hindu cycle of transmigration would seem more congenial to such a wanderer and explorer.

C. ELIOT.

AUTHOR'S PREFACE

Having been resident for a considerable time in Zanzibar, I had the opportunity of becoming closely acquainted with the hero of this work, and I succeeded in inducing him to recount the story of his life, which seemed to me of interest in view of the important part which he has played in the history of African exploration. His descriptions were set down by him in Swahili in Arabic characters, and by me transcribed into Roman script, in which form they appeared, together with a German translation, in the 'Proceedings of the Institute of Oriental Languages,' Part III, fifth and sixth yearly issues.

In the preface of that study I pointed out that its publication in that place primarily served a linguistic purpose, and announced that I intended to work up the material furnished me by Tippu Tip into a work on his life which should be generally intelligible.

The present book is the carrying out of that announcement. Owing to urgent professional work, its publication has been delayed longer than I anticipated. Within the framework of the life-history of a prominent personality it has been my object to lay before the reader, even though unfamiliar with African affairs, a picture of the varying fortunes of the Dark Continent before it gradually fell into European hands. The historical introduction in the first chapter may seem to many far-fetched, yet in the interest of the work as a whole I was loth to omit it. Should any reader find it wearisome, I beg him to begin at the second chapter, but whoever does not shrink from the trouble of reading it through will find in it many a hint which will make the subsequent descriptions more comprehensible.

Before the work leaves my hands I feel it my duty to express my thanks to all those who have afforded me their counsel and co-operation during its compilation.

THE AUTHOR.

ZANZIBAR,
September, 1903.

[The death of Tippu Tip since the original edition was published has necessitated the addition of a few words by the author, which will be found on page 132.]

Zanzibar Stone Town

CHAPTER 1

HISTORICAL INTRODUCTION: EAST AFRICA UP TO THE REIGN OF SEYYID SAID (1806-1856)

'Marche toujours: un monde est lá.'-GUILLAIN.

When, about the middle of the last century, the attention of a wider circle was directed to the quarter which people were accustomed to call the Dark Continent, probably very few of those who heard of the astounding discoveries of European travellers-of snowy mountains and vast lakes at the Equator-realized that thousands of years ago daring navigators had directed their course to that very East Coast which in our day was to be the starting-point of the assault on the secrets of the new region. No less an authority than the father of history, Herodotus, informs us that even in primeval times Phoenician fishermen circumnavigated the southern extremity of Africa. True, those accounts are confused, and what they relate is not always to be reconciled with the geographical knowledge of our days; yet as every echo is the reverberation of a real voice so there is no fable so foolish but some grain of truth is contained in it. And the mighty ruins of Mashonaland, discovered a few decades ago, and recently more thoroughly explored by Carl Peters, do indeed tell in forcible language of primeval civilization on the East Coast of Africa. We may take it that the Phoenicians and Assyrians, those pioneers of maritime commerce, sowed and reaped here; and even the mysterious land of Ophir, to which, according to the old Testament narrative, King Hiram sent his ocean-going ships,* seems to assume palpable form. But over it all floats the veil of the fabulous, which the inquirer may here and there softly lift, but which he can never quite tear away from the stony countenance of the Sphinx, that inexorable guardian of primeval secrets.

In all this chaos of legends and fables only this fact remains established-that these regions were known to the oldest seafaring peoples, just as these knew the Indian Peninsula as long ago as two thousand years before Christ. One of the oldest historical documents we possess concerning the geography of East Africa is the 'Periplus of the Erythraean Sea,'† which appeared at the beginning of our era, and is probably wrongly ascribed to Arrian of Nicodemia (who lived early in the 2nd century), which tells of a great city called Raphta, whose site can indeed be no longer determined, but which in the opinion of most commentators must havelain between the present coastal towns of Mombasa and Mozambique. A later proof of the connection of East Africa with the Arabian Peninsula is furnished by the fact that in the South Arabian religious wars of the eighth century African slaves formed a considerable portion of the armies engaged.* Their number and power increased so much that a hundred years later they were able to enter on a conflict with their oppressors. In 869 a fierce servile war broke out, which, starting from Basra, devastated South Iraq and Kurdistan for fourteen years, and threatened to overthrow the Arab domination there. The leader of the rebels was the Arab Ali bin Mohammed, nicknamed El Khabith (the Monster). His hordes were called the Zeng, a word equivalent to the Zingis of the Greeks, which was used to designate the East Coast and its inhabitants, and which still survives in the word Zanzibar (Arabic *Zengibar* = Land of the Zeng).

While, then, we have such clear proof that African natives were carried off in masses as slaves to more northerly countries, on the other hand, political conditions in these regions in the seventh and following centuries were such as could not fail to favour migration to the new regions. In 630 Mohammed had imposed his doctrines and political influence on the city of Mecca, from which he had had to flee eight years before; two years later all Arabia lay at his feet. Under his successors-Abu Bekr, Omar, and Othman-Islam began that brilliant career of victory which ended with the subjugation of Southern Persia, Syria, Egypt, and the whole of North Africa. The assassination of Othman in the year 656 gave the first blow* to the creed which had till then seemed invincible, and sowed the first seed of a fratricidal quarrel which has lasted ever since. Othman's behaviour had shown him to be an unworthy successor of the Prophet, and he fell by the dagger of fanatics. Ali, the cousin and son-in-law of the Prophet, was legally chosen as his successor, but was not recognised by Othman's adherents, who accused him of complicity in the murder of Othman. Moawija was hoisted on the shield by them. Several sanguinary battles were followed in 657 by an armistice, and it was decided to refer to a court of arbitration the question who should be Khalif. But not only was no agreement arrived at: the hoped-for remedy itself proved a source of fresh discord. The very acceptance of the armistice was a sin against the Koran, which forbids making terms with rebels against God's will, and enjoins war to the knife against them. All who implicitly followed the divine precepts separated from the adherents of Ali, and under the name of Kharigites, or Separatists, took up the struggle withthose who had rebelled against God's word. In the famous Battle of Nahrawan (658) they were slain almost to a man, but their belief did not perish with them.In 661 a Kharigite murdered Ali, whose son gave up his claims to Moawija, and he in turn became the object of a desperate feud on the part of the Kharigites, which was fatal to the latter. Yet, despite these reverses, the sect survived, and founded a new State in

---

*1 Kings ix., x.

† Compare also for what follows Guillain, 'Documents sur l'Histoire, la Géographie et la Commerce de l'Afrique Orientale' (Paris, 1856), vol. i., p. 81, and Strandes, 'Portugesienzeit in Deutsch-und Englisch-Ostafrika' (Berlin, 1899), p. 81 et seq.

*Müller, 'Der Islam in Morgen-und Abendland,' Berlin, 1885, vol.i., p. 583 et seq.

*Sachau, 'Religiöse Anschauungen der Ibaditischen Muhamedaner,' in the *Mitteilungen des Semmais für Orientalische Sprachen*, Berlin, 1898.

Oman, whose inhabitants were later to be the lords of East Africa; and such, with their old inflexible religion, they have in a certain sense remained to the present day, greatly as the last decades have undermined their domination.

It is in accordance with human nature that internal dissensions such as those described above should favour migration to peaceful regions. That such actually took place to the East Coast one or two centuries later is established by an old Arab chronicle, which fell into the hands of the Portuguese at the taking of Kilwa in 1505.

This chronicle lays no claim to accuracy, especially in its earlier parts. It sets forth that the first Arab settlers in East Africa were followers of Said, a son of Hussein, the great-grandson of the Prophet. In it they are designated by the Arabic expression 'ummet Said,' which has been corrupted by later writers into 'Emosaides.' These Emosaides are said to have founded no permanent towns, but merely to have lived together for mutual protection. It was not till a century later, apparently, that the first Moslem towns were founded, and the first steps thus taken towards subjecting the littoral. About A.D. 900, the chronicle relates, a band of Arabs, driven out by the state of affairs at home, fled from the town of EL Hasa, on the Persian Gulf, and in three ships, under the leadership of nine brothers, reached the Somali coast, where they founded the towns of Mogadishu and Brawa. A further migration-a Persian one this time-followed, according to the chronicle, some seventy years later. It seems that Ali, a son of Sultan Hassan, of Persia, left his home in Shiraz owing to family dissensions. Attracted by stories of the gold which abounded in Africa, he sailed from Ormuz with two ships for the settlements mentioned; but as he could not get on with the Arabs, he went further south, and founded the city of Kilwa, which later attained to great prosperity. A second chronicle of Kilwa that has come down to us also ascribes the founding of the city to Ali, although it varies in details from the version of the first chronicle. According to the first of the two chronicles Ali's son Mohammed subsequently founded Mombasa, a statement confirmed by a still extant chronicle of the latter city-at least, in so far that, according to it, the oldest rulers of the city were sheikhs from Shiraz.

The people to-day still preserve the memory of an earlier Persian immigration; and from many details, into which this is not the place to enter, it may be taken for certain that for a longtime Shirazi families, with a culture far in advance of the present
Arab civilization, ruled the East Coast, without driving away by their presence the Arabs previously settled there, who probably were always numerically superior to them. A trace of such coexistence of Arab and Shirazi domination continued in Zanzibar until lately. The island had long been in possession of the Arabs, and when Said, Sultan of Muscat, transferred his capital there in 1832, could be regarded as a wholly Arab country. Nevertheless, there reigned side by side with this Sultan, scarcely three hours' journey from his capital, perfectly undisturbed, and without a sign of dependence, under the designation of *Mwinyi Mkuu* (Great Lord), a ruler of undoubted Shirazi descent, whom the original inhabitants of the islands, the Wahadimu and Watambatu, regarded as their legitimate sovereign. This extraordinary state of things did not cease till the death, in 1856, of the last scion of that family. His grave lies close before the palace of the Arab Sultan (in the grounds of the German club). How matters developed further on the East Coast cannot be ascertained from

the existing chronicles. After the manner of all Arabs records, they give long-winded genealogical tables, which have no interest for posterity, and from which the student can gather but little as to the degree of civilization prevailing at various times. All that need be dwelt on is that towards the end of the twelfth century there appears to have been at Kilwa a ruler of the name of Hassan, who, during a reign of eighteen years, brought his city to a high state of prosperity, and made it the mistress of trade as far down as Sofala. He is said also to have erected a large fortress and many stone buildings.

Mogadishu also must at that time have been an important town, as may be gathered from two inscriptions, dated respectively 1238 and 1269, preserved there. This tallies with other accounts, according to which trade in India, as in the whole Arabian Sea, was at that time particularly flourishing. Even the Chinese, who had long carried on a brisk traffic with India, came to East Africa soon after.

Marco Polo (c.1254 - c.1324) informs us that the Emperor of China sent a whole Chinese fleet on a voyage of discovery to Madagascar, and from later Chinese sources it appears that Chinese junks visited Mogadishu. The connection of this ancient civilized nation with our coast is confirmed by the finding of Chinese coins at Kilwa and Mogadishu. The coins range from the sixth to the twelfth centuries of our era.

A new epoch was inaugurated for East Africa with the voyages of discovery of the Portuguese, beginning with the circumnavigation of the southern extremity of the continent by Bartholomew Diaz (1487) and the voyage to India of Vasco da Gama(1497-1502). From that time on these lands are brought geographically nearer to us. In what stage the Portuguese then found Semitic culture on the East Coast, whether just at its acme or already beginning to decline, can hardly be determined; at any rate, their narratives are full of wonder at what they saw, which certainly must have been very different from what they were accustomed to see on the uncivilized West Coast. Along the whole coast, from Sofala to India, an extensive traffic was carried on, especially in gold and clothing material of all kinds. The inhabitants were white and black Moors (Arabs and Swahili); both races were well clad and richly decked with gold and jewels. Soon, by conquest or treachery, the whole coast became a Portuguese possession. But as yet only the coast is spoken of. There is no talk of further penetration into the interior-rather, nothing appears to be known of the country beyond the walls of the fortified settlements. They content themselves with sucking the goodness out of the country from there. The Portuguese were far worse colonists then the Arabs. Their rule bore within it the seed of death, and two hundred years later no trace of Portuguese conquest remained on African soil. They left nothing distinctive behind them in the country; the towns which they found prospering are in ruins, and only here and there a stone inscription or a cannon buried in the sand of the shore reminds us that centuries ago the longvanished might of a European nation was displayed here.

After the common enemy had been finally driven away there arose, in the second half of the eighteenth century, an internecine strife between the two Arab races, which again brought serious calamity on the country and ended in the final victory of the Busaid dynasty, the rulers of that Oman already spoken of, a small and wretched little country in the north-east corner Arabia. Under Sultan Said (1804-1856) a new period of prosperity set in for East Africa. As a land of sixteen this talented and unscrupulous ruler deposed his uncle, Kis bin Ahmed, from the throne of Oman; a few years later his last enemies in Mombasa had been overthrown by cunning or by force of arms, and when at length, in 1832, he transferred his capital to Zanzibar, a vast realm extending from the north-east extremity of Arabia right down the east coast as far as Cape Delgado was united under his sceptre.

True, here again it is only the coasts of the East African mainland on which a direct political influence is exercised, but individual attempts to penetrate into the interior and secure its treasures have already begun. The gold of Sofala has fallen into oblivion, but new objects of value have taken its place. The cultivation of cloves, which had become familiar in Mauritius, has been introduced in Zanzibar, and in an astonishingly short time conquers that island and Pemba, to which it still gives its stamp. Now, for the working of the clove plantations labour is needed, and this is furnished in ample measure by the dark interior. Such of it as cannot be utilized in the broad plantations is exported, as was the case over a thousand years before, to the North, to Arabia and the countries on the Persian Gulf, and brings rich profits to the slave-hunters and middlemen, and not less to the ruler of the country, who levies a considerable poll-tax on every slave brought to Zanzibar.

A further important article of commerce is ivory, the thirst for which entices men further and further into regions where the value of the precious tusk is not yet known, and for a piece of bright-coloured fabric any amount can be obtained in exchange from the inexperienced natives, unless the trader prefers to take it from them by force. Gradually, too, folks find their way to the great lakes. On the route to Lake Tanganyika the town of Tabora has become an *entrepot*, where a great number of Arabs and Indian traders have taken up their abode, and are ruled by the Vali, the Sultan's own representative, who administers justice there in the name of his master and is dependent on his commands. On the lake itself flourishes the town of Ujiji, which again is subject to the Sultan. In short, a new life has awoken trade reaches a high pitch of prosperity, and whoever has the daring necessary to face a journey into the interior, with its dangers, can, in a short space of time, become a rich man.

Man counting Ivory

CHAPTER II

THE FIRST JOURNEYS OF TIPPU TIP

'What from thy fathers thou inherit'st
That earn and make indeed thine own.'
GOETHE: *Faust.*

The commencement of the journeys undertaken by daring slave- and ivory-hunters, which led to the ultimate founding of Tabora and Ujiji, dates back to a far earlier period, of course, than the reign of Said just described. The first adventurers must have found what they sought-viz. slaves and ivory-in the neighbourhood of the coast. After the nearer districts had been depopulated or the survivors grown too strong for violence and too artful in trading, they gradually advanced further and further; and he who was brave enough to push forward into unknown tracts always found in the boundless interior a new sphere to which no Arab had penetrated before him, and which he, as the first comer, could exploit. If the inhabitants were warlike and he could not rely on his own strength-a certain display of force was always an essential in untried regions-the traveller could resort to the way of diplomatic manoeuvring in peaceful trade and wheedle out of the inexperienced savages the precious ivory, whose value they did not know, at a cheap rate, and could also barter a few pieces of coloured fabric for a whole crowd of slaves. If, on the contrary, natives were weak and victory seemed certain, a shorter procedure was adopted. Peaceful hamlets were surprised and plundered, and such of the natives as could be captured were carried off as slaves. In this fashion many an Arab who went forth a poor man must have returned home wealthy, and thereby the tales he told or the display of his wealth spread the news that in East Africa, with a little audacity, a man might soon become rich. The success of the first comers constantly incited fresh adventurers to seek fortune in these unknown regions.

It was this spirit of adventure that about the middle of the last century led a member of a respected Muscat family, Juma bin Mohammed el Nebhani, to the gainful coast of East Africa. He settled at Mbwa Maji, a small village to the south of the present German capital of Dar es Salaam. There he married a an African woman, who bore him three children-a son named Mohammed and two daughters, the eldest called Mwana Arabu. Having grown rich, he returned to his home at Muscat with his son, who had meanwhile grown up, to end his days there. His son, however, went back to East Africa, this time in company with Rajab bin Mohammed bin Said el Murgebi, the great-grand-father of our hero. To him he gave in marriage his sister Mwana Arabu, who had remained behind at Mbwa Maji, and from this union sprang Juma bin Rajab, an enterprising leader of caravans, who, by daring raids to Tabora and Lake Tanganyika, was already winning great influence.

Through him Mwura, grandfather of the afterwards so much dreaded bandit Mirambo, became Sultan of Ujoa, a small tract lying west of Uriakuru. Later on he travelled together with his son Mohammed, Tippu Tip's father, who raised himself still further by an advantageous marriage. Fundi Kira, the then powerful Sultan of Tabora, gave him his daughter Karunde to wife. But as the Moslem is allowed to have four wives-the number of concubines whom he may choose as well from among his slaves is unlimited, and depends entirely on the means of the individual-he married besides at Zanzibar the daughter of a respected and prosperous Muscat family, Bint Habib bin Bushir, of the clan of Wardi, who had previously been married to her relative Masoud bin Mohammed, but had been divorced by him-a common occurrence among Arabs.

From this new marriage sprang Hamed bin Mohammed, surnamed Tippu Tip. He was bornat the *shamba* of Kwarara, in Zanzibar, belonging to a relative of his mother's. His bringing up was, in accordance with Arab custom, the simplest conceivable. At about six years of age he was handed over to an ignorant tutor to learn reading and writing by the help of the Koran. After the attempt had failed in the case of the first teacher, he was entrusted to a second, who, when the usual period of learning was at an end, dismissed him as an 'educated man.' As he grew up he made himself as useful as he could on his mother's property; at sixteen he set out on his first journey. Together with some relatives on his mother's side, among them his half-brother Bushir bin Habib, he travelled the opposite coast, trading in copal, at first on a small scale, as suited his slender credit.

At eighteen he was summoned by his father, who usually lived at Tabora, but came now and again to the coast, to undertake a great journey. At Ugangi, north-east of Lake Nyassa, they traded in ivory and slaves, selling their acquisitions later on at Zanzibar. When the father returned to Tabora he took his son with him. On the way the latter was attacked by the smallpox, a disease which never quite dies out in East Africa, and has left its cruel mark on many a African and Arab face. Thus the unhappy pretender to the throne, Seyyid Khalid, son of the powerful Sultan Bargash, who lives at Dar-es-salaam, has his fine Oriental features woefully disfigured by it. The disease, strange to say, has left no visible traces on Tippu Tip; his beauty would have suffered no loss even if it had, for, apart from the negative advantage of having no pock-marks, Tippu Tip can certainly not claim to be an Adonis. His face shows the thorough African type, which is the more remarkable as he comes of a good Arab family, and his pedigree was only defaced by his grandmother on the father's side, who was an African woman. None the less, he may call himself an Arab, for folks only ask about the origin of the father. The child of the blackest slave-woman counts for as much as the offspring of a princess if it is only born in legitimate wedlock. And, in spite of its easy dissolution, every matrimonial alliance of a Moslem with any of his female slaves is legitimate.

But to return to our chronological narrative. In Unyanyembe, the country of Tippu Tip's father, a stay of only two months was made; then the party went on, accompanied by a goodly band of Arabs, to Ujiji, on Lake Tanganyika. Here, however, they found the prices of ivory unfavourable, so most of the Arabs determined to try their luck on the west side of Lake Tanganyika, in Urua. Old Mohammed was recalled to Tabora by his duties as ruler, so he commissioned his son to trade for him in the new country, taking with him the objects of barter that were current there-pearls and mussels. But he was to travel under the supervision of an experienced man of the coast. Here the independent temper of the young merchant showed itself for the first time. Though hardly eighteen, he indignantly rejected the suggestion that he should carry on his business under the control of another. 'If you want to trust your wares to this Swahili, and I am to be under him, it is better I should go back with you.' The old man put it to him that he was still young and did not know trade in Urua; gladly as he would have entrusted the guidance of the caravan to him, he (Tippu Tip) must really give way this time. But Tippu Tip remained obdurate, declaring that he must try it once; if things went wrong, in future his father might trust his affairs to whom he pleased. He thus obtained his father's permission, and set out on his journey. In great canoes-the hollowed-out trunks of mighty trees, such as only the primeval forest produces-they crossed Lake Tanganyika in primitive fashion.

It was a numerous band which travelled towards the little-known West: not less than twenty Arabs were eager to open up fresh sources of profit in the country. They reached the adobe of Mwagu Tambu, a Sultan of friendly disposition. The traffic in ivory was not exceptional, but it was tolerable. Large tusks were dear, small ones comparatively cheap. While the other Arabs purchased the dearer large tusks, Tippu Tip decided to buy the smaller specimens, and in doing so made a lucky speculation, as was shown later on the coast.

As a rule large tusks, be it said, are more expensive, and of these, again, the soft ones, as being easier to work, are from 20 to 30 per cent. dearer than the hard ones.* Among the soft tusks the following distinctions are made: Large tusks of best quality and slightly curved, suitable for making billiard-balls, have been quoted of late years at from 114 to 145 dollars (£17 to £23) per *frasila* (35 pounds). The next best kind, which is particularly suitable for piano keys, is called, because it is principally exported to Europe, 'Bab Ulaya,' and of late years has fetched from 105 to 130 dollars (£15 to £20) per *frasila*. A third kind is exported India, and is therefore called 'Bab Cutch,' and is the making of arm and leg rings. It fetches from 95 to 113 dollars (£14 to £17). Small tusks, which are obtained from the younger elephants, are relatively much cheaper, yet they may also, under certain circumstances, reach high prices. As they are often used as ornaments when mounted in silver, the attractiveness of their shape and the fancy of the purchaser are the chief factors in determining their price. It is thus quite intelligible that Tippu Tip was lucky in his speculation in small tusks; he would have been even more successful with them today, as in order to spare the breed of elephants, both the German and the British Governments have forbidden the shooting of young elephants.

After finishing their business they came on the way back to Mtoa, on the western shore of Lake Tanganyika. Here they heard of great changes that had taken place mean

---

Cf. **the Trade Reports for at home and abroad, separately published by the German Ministry of the Interior, Series III., No.1, December, 1899.**

while in their new home, Unyanyembe. Fundikira, the Sultan of Tabora, was dead, and the Overlord of the country had set up his nephew, Mnywa Sere (the 'Tembo-drinker'), as his successor. This aggrieved another relative, Mkasiva, who, being nearer to the throne, made preparations to wrest from the other his usurped sovereignty. Mnywa Sere did not wait to be attacked, but tried to crush his opponent before he grew too strong. A twenty days' conflict, however, resulted indecisively. He then turned for help to old Mohammed, whom he induced by rich presents of ivory to support him with a great number of Arabs and their dependents. Within a month Mkasiva was decisively routed, a great portion of his followers killed, and others taken prisoners, while he himself escaped with difficulty to Uriankuru.

This cheaply-earned victory went to the 'Tembo-drinker's' head, so that he began to oppress his former helpers, primarily in the shape of 'hongo' or toll, an institution to which the chiefs in the interior, when they were strong enough, always resorted to enrich themselves at the expense of passing caravans. Where there was no help for it, people put up with this, only the contribution had to be kept within reasonable bounds. With Mnywa Sere this was not the case: he made very large demands, and the business was highly profitable, for the immigration of Arabs was about this time particularly great, favoured by the political events in Zanzibar, which drove a great number of them to leave their homes. In 1856 Seyyid* Said, the powerful Sultan, had died; he was the last of his race to unite the dominions in East Africa and Oman under one sceptre. A great lover of women, he had owned a splendid harem, from which had sprung some twenty sons, besides numerous daughters. The eldest, Thueni, took the reins in Oman; in Zanzibar Majid ascended the throne, much to the grief of his next brother, afterwards Sultan Bargash, who would have liked to become ruler himself. After various smaller intrigues, he made in 1859 a determined attempt to overthrow Seyyid Majid.

In the interior of the island, some four hours' journey from the city, lies a country-seat, to which Said, who was greatly under French influence, had given the name of Marseilles. Now that the importance of France in Zanzibar has diminished people have forgotten the foreign title, and gone back to the old name Machui, which signifies something like 'in the wilderness.' Here Bargash had assembled his forces, after an attempt in the city had failed. Majid, who was too weak to contend with Bargash alone, called to his aid the English, who placed a detachment of sailors at his disposal. An inglorious attack, in which the Sultan's troops and the English contended for the lead-the wrong way around-failed indeed, yet so far alarmed Bargash that he stole away in the night and concluded peace. He was exiled to Bombay, and his adherents were likewise banished or imprisoned, those that were well-to-do being further punished with confiscations of property, an arrangement as painful to the sufferer as gratifying to the inflicter. Greatly injured in this way, and still not secure against Majid's vengeance, many Arabs migrated, to seek a new home in the

---

*'Seyyid' signifies 'lord,' and is the attribute of the Sultan and his belongings. 'Said,' with a guttural sound before the *i*, is a proper name, and means 'lucky.' In Swahili pronunciation the two words sound almost alike, and so they are mostly wrongly reproduced by European writers.

interior, chiefly at Tabora and on Lake Tanganyika. Descendants of the fugitives of that day are still numerous at Tabora.

To these haughty Arabs it was, of course, monstrous to endure the oppression of a 'Shensi'-a savage-and so the bitterness against Mnywa Sere grew more and more; yet no one dared undertake anything against the favourite of old Mohammed. At length the tyrant himself went too far by daring to have Karunde's uncle and mother murdered. If Mohammed had been a Westerner and a reader of 'Fliegende Blatter,' he might, perhaps, have regarded the doing away with his mother-in-law as a friendly action; but, being an Oriental, he fell into a passion over this interference in his family affairs, and planned revenge. He was at Ituru-the settlement belonging to him in the immediate neighbourhood of Tabora-when he learnt the news of the outrage. The Arabs living there were only too ready to follow him in arms. 'We have long been inclined,' they declared, 'to strike the tyrant; it only out of consideration for you that we have put up with his oppressions.' Immediately the plan of action was framed. It was proposed to band together all the Arabs resident in the district, to wait for the coming of Tippu Tip and his companions, which was expected shortly, and in the meantime to send secretly to Mkasiva, whom it was proposed to draw out of concealment, and set up as the successor of Mnywa Sere. This last mission was undertaken by the Arab Salum bin Sef el Bahari. In the remaining preparations the most prominent was taken by Thenei bin Amur, a 'Besar'-*i.e.,* an Arab from Oman, only not of pure blood, but the issue of the slave caste. These 'Besars' as a rule occupy a subordinate position socially as compared with the full-blooded Arabs, the 'Kubails,' whom they have to address as 'Hebabi,' or 'Lord'; but often they are far superior to them in intelligence, and attain to considerable wealth-an advantage which, as money everywhere is in good repute, in its turn helps to raise their importance. Thenei was one of these honourable exceptions to his class, and enjoyed great consideration among the Arabs. His proposal that all Arabs should assemble at one place, and thus stand prepared for a possible sudden attack by Mnywa Sere, was readily adopted, the more so as he closed his instructions with the pithy comment: 'He who does not hearken to me understands nothing of the conduct of war; let him hereafter, if things go wrong, blame not me, but himself' (from the Koran: Sura Ibrahim, xiv. 27).

The place of assembly appointed was the hamlet of Kwihara, not far from Tabora, where within twelve days some 300 to 400 Arabs with their attendants were gathered. Tippu Tip with his men also arrived at this stage of the preparations, and took up his quarters with Sultan bin Ali, the chief of Kwihara. The latter had as yet no idea of the plan of campaign, and may well have been astonished to find such a number of guests on his hands. With true Arab hospitality, however, he set his best before them; for, according to custom, the host may not ask till the third day what brings the stranger to him. But presumably they initiated him before that.

It all but went badly with them as they were feasting at Kwihara, for Mnywa Sere had got wind of their intentions, and endeavoured to frustrate them by attacking first. There lived at Tabora an Indian trader, Musa, surnamed the Handsome, who some years before, following the migration westward, had come to the country, in company with a compatriot who had since died, to promote civilization by the sale of brandy and other modern requirements. One of his principal customers was Mnywa Sere, who bartered the to him valueless ivory with the ingenious middleman for the marvels of European and Indian industry.

At this time messengers from the Sultan had just come on matters of business to the Indian. As his interests required, the handsome Musa at once gave these people the necessary hints. 'The Arabs are planning something against your Sultan. They have assembled at Kwihara, at Sultan bin Ali's, and are only waiting for Mkasiva, whom they mean to set up as the new Sultan.' In all haste the messengers conveyed the weighty news to their master, who in his first eagerness formed the sensible resolution to be the first in the field, and by an immediate attack on the Arabs loitering at Kwihara put a speedy end to the war; but, with the usual recklessness of the African, in the end he allowed himself to be persuaded by his indolent followers to wait till he was attacked. 'One could not tell as yet whether the whole thing was not a fraud. And even if it was true, he would by-and-by make child's play of conquering the Arabs.' He had at that time, Tippu Tip declares, a large force. 'If he had come it would have been most dangerous for us, and our food would probably have never tasted sweet to us again.'

At length Mkasiva arrived. The war for which such ample preparations had been made began. For three months they ravaged, burned, and plundered; and then the power of the 'Tembo-drinker' was broken. He himself escaped, and Mkasiva became Sultan. Soon after the war Tippu Tip returned to the coast.

CHAPTER III

JOURNEY TO ITAHUA

He ever was a wicked wight;
Him Heaven's vengeance smote aright.'
F. KIND: *Freischütz.*

At Zanzibar Tippu Tip first carried out certain commissions of his father's: he sold his ivory and sent him further articles of barter in the interior. He himself did not for the present return to Unyanzembe, but began to travel on his own account. As he naturally, as a young beginner, had but scanty credit-he had to borrow money in sums of from one to a thousand dollars-he contented himself for the time with smaller undertakings; but as he succeeded in these he extended his expeditions further into the interior, and at last undertook a longer journey into the Lake Tanganyika districts, which brought him in much ivory and probably many slaves as well. When he returned from this tour to Zanzibar, twelve years had passed since his first trip to Tabora. In that time he had become a rich man.

Things had not gone so well with his young halfbrother and friend, Mohammed bin Masoud el Wardi, whom now for the first time he saw again in their home after a long separation. In the meantime he had tried his luck in another way. He had 'traded,' as it is very discreetly styled in Tippu Tip's jottings, between Ngao, the southern coast district of our colony, and the Benadir coast. On my asking further the nature of this trading, Tippu Tip had to own with a smirk that his brother had undertaken slave-hunts in the south, and sold his booty in more northerly regions. He had not grown rich from it, for his friend Mohammed bin Said el Herthi, with whom he had been in partnership in the business, had recklessly squandered all the takings, and left nothing over for him. He therefore gladly joined his brother, who was already beginning to be famous, when the latter again started for the interior. To be sure, he could contribute as yet only on a small scale, for it was not possible for him to borrow more than 5,000 dollars.

Tippu Tip, on the other hand, started with goods to the value of 30,000 dollars, though he had to search diligently for people who would give him credit. He left twenty creditors behind oscillating between fear and hope. It was no light matter, in view of the uncertain conditions, to stake much money on a caravan for the interior. How many of them never came back again! Either the whole was wiped out by savages or the leader died, and all the property was made away with by his unskilful or faithless followers. In many cases, too, the debtor preferred, instead of abiding by his obligations in Zanzibar, to lead a showy life in the interior with other people's money. Wissmann, in his crossing of

Africa in 1883, encountered such a worthy* in Nyangwe. On the other hand, the profit was all the greater when a debtor came back richly laden from the interior. The Indians keep a good tally; they are not apt to forget anything; indeed, they are more likely to enter an item twice over to make sure. And the Arab, to whom book-keeping is an abomination-the acknowledgment of a debt is the only document he ever keeps-pays willingly, provided he has the means, in order to keep up his credit. He will need the cashbox of his Indian business friend for his next expedition. Of those who enter into such speculations, the Swahili say, 'Wanabahatisha sana '('They tempt Fortune').

So the journey began, and not under very favourable auspices. On the mainland there was a famine. In order not to pass through quite impoverished districts, Tippu Tip chose, instead of the ordinary route by Usagara and Ugogo, the more southerly one by Urori, which also, as being little used, was the richer in ivory. But the Wanyamwezi-the tribe that usually furnishes the carriers (and very good ones)-declined to follow him there. The African is in the highest degree conservative. What runs counter to *dasturi*, or ancient custom, is distasteful to him. The Wanyamwezi had been used in former journeys always to pass through Usagara and then through their native country, and now all of a sudden it was to be through Urori, a quite unknown region. They were not going to agree to that!

Then-a blessing in disguise-the famine came to the rescue in the difficulty. The Wasaramo, a tribe which usually would not condescend to porter's work, found themselves compelled by hard times to adopt that profitable means of livelihood. Two hundred men were speedily enlisted, and they were not dear. In addition to their keep, they got for the whole journey, which would probably last whole years, 10 dollars-*i.e.*, at the present rate, about 30 marks. From a fourth to a third of this was given to them beforehand. The journey began from Mbwa Maji, the place already mentioned, on the coast south of Dar-es-Salaam, at first in a southerly direction towards Rufiji. They crossed the little river Mbezi, and in three days reached Mkamba, where a halt was called, that they might equip themselves for a six days' journey through districts devoid of food.

When the drum of the caravan sounded on the day appointed for the start, an unpleasant surprise was in store, which has brought many an African traveller to despair. The porters, delighted with their advance and in happy possession of provisions for six days, had made off in a body. The *ngoma* might resound as loudly as it would, not a carrier appeared. The men who were sent to the various quarters of the Wasaramo-of course, the whole 700 had not found shelter in one place, but had housed themselves in the neighbouring villages, sixty men to a village-returned, unsuccessful; no one came. 'Then my reason deserted me,' writes Tippu Tip himself. He seems, however, to have been still capable of sound deliberation, for he at once called out his men, and proceeded with eighty guns back along the way he had come. They marched till dark, then simply bivouacked on the high-road, and the next morning reached the first abodes of the Wasaramo.

The fugitives had, it is true, not yet arrived, but what did that matter to the Arab

---

*Abed bin Salem. *Cf.* Wissmann, I Unter Deutscher Flagge quer durch Afrika,' Berlin, 1889, pp. 181, 182.

sense of justice? The whole tribe had to pay for the misdeeds of its sons. Quickly enough 200 people were seized and put in irons. Resistance to the armed Swahilis was not to be thought of. So they moved, plundering and burning, from place to place, and within five days 800 people had been taken captive. The promptness with which Tippu Tip had acted earned him the title of 'Kingugwa chui'-*i.e.*, the 'Leopard,' who breaks in now here, now there.

On being seized, they were temporarily secured in wooden yokes, such as every slave-hunter used, and taken to Mkamba, where an Indian merchant Banyane Hila, lived. From him Tippu Tip procured iron rods and had chains forged of them by workmen whom he had taken with him expressly for that purpose. In these he put the involuntary carriers, and with them finally began his march. To ensure that no one should escape, he himself brought up the rear; at the head marched his brother, Mohammed bin Masoud, whose powerful military following earned him among the Shensis the name of 'Kumbakumba,' 'the Gatherer of Everything.'

Thus they reached Urori, where the powerful Sultan Merere was then reigning. He had formerly been friendly to the Arabs, but later, being incensed at the wanton acts of travellers, changed his policy and attacked various caravans of his former friends. A certain Amran bin Masoud, one of the Arabs who had fled after the unsuccessful attempt of Bargash, had avenged his compatriots on him, and so far humbled him that he was willing to purchase peace by a yearly payment of a hundred tusks. The victor would not agree to this. Later the fortune of war changed: Amran himself was defeated and lost his life in the conflict.

When Tippu Tip came there the country had just been reopened to peaceful traffic, and the conditions of trade were the most favourable conceivable. For from twelve to fifteen garments a *frasila* of ivory was to be had. It could be purchased also for a *frasila* of spices or a chest of soap, or for 15 pounds of powder. This happy state of trade caused Tippu Tip to leave one of his men behind in the country, to carry on business on his account, to whom he entrusted goods to the value of 6,000 dollars. He himself proceeded with the bulk of the caravan to Ruemba, where he was amicably received by the Sultan, but was unable to make any profitable bargains. This was mostly the case. Where the Arabs were wanted they were well received, but there was nothing profitable to be gained by them.

Then Tippu Tip resolved to go to Itahua, a country which then had a very bad reputation. A Sultan ruled there named Nsama, a powerful and most bloodthirsty chief, from whom all Arabs who had hitherto entered his territory had had a bad experience. Tippu Tip left his brother Mohammed bin Masoud behind at Ruemba with 15 guns, and himself marched with 105 guns through Urunga to the dreaded country. Everywhere on the way the natives endeavoured to hold him back by tales of Nsama's power and cruelty. Moreover, an old Arab named Amer bin Said esh Shaqsi, who had spent years in the country, frightened him with an account of an expedition which he had made a considerable time ago with other Arabs, but from which very few had returned alive. But our wanderer was powerfully attracted to this rich country, for all accounts agreed in affirming that there were untold treasures of ivory there. So he and his men crossed the stream which forms the boundary between Urungu and Itahua.

Immediately on entering the country he acquired an idea of its wealth. They marched through luxuriant plantations from one populous township to another, and the natives were immoderately haughty towards the intruders. This was no wonder, for only a short time before they had given proof of their power. The robber tribe of the Wangoni, a terror to all adjacent countries, had endeavoured to surprise Nsama's powerful realm as well, but had been driven off with bloody sconces. Their defeat had contributed to heighten the repute of Nsama's invincibility. The neighbouring tribes had long been tributary to him, Ruemba and Urungu even the nearer townships of the great central African kingdom of Urua paid him contributions. After six days' march the caravan reached a mountain, at the foot of which was built a great city, Nsama's capital. Like all East African towns in old days, and many even now, it was strongly fortified with palisades, thorn-hedges and trenches.* Tippu Tip pitched his camp outside the city on a spot assigned to him by Nsama's people. The next morning he with the other Arabs was summoned before the Sultan. As to the receptions and the events which followed it, we will allow him to give his own account.

'We went and took him such and such garments as a present. He was then a very old man, between eighty-six and ninety. He said to his attendants: "Carry me, so that I may show them the ivory." Then he was carried on their shoulders, and showed us a very great stock of ivory in the storehouses. Thereupon I said to him: "Sultan, will you not give us two tusks?" Then he suddenly began to abuse me, and we could see that all the goods we had given the fellow were a dead loss. To the other Sultans we gave but few goods, and they used to give us each two or three tusks, while this man, to whom we had given a large present, abused me.

'We took our leave and went to our camp. The next morning he sent us a messenger to summon us. We were to go into his city; all Arabs were sent for. People were to come with us, too, to carry away the ivory. But he held his soldiers in readiness in great numbers, and we knew nothing of it. We went to the number of twenty, and took ten of our slaves with us. When we got there I, who was walking in front, was hit by three arrows-two hit me full on, the other more slightly. A young man named Said bin Sef el Maamri was also wounded by a well-aimed arrow, and two slaves were wounded by arrows, and died at once. But we bad our guns at the ready, loaded with bullets and biggish shot, and they were standing in separate groups. At a shot they fell like birds. When our guns began to crackle 200 people fell at once; others were trampled down, and so died. They hurriedly took to flight. Within an hour over 1,000 fell. On our side only the two slaves and we two were wounded, and the town was really very large. So they were routed and fled. They took their Sultan with them. At last, by two o'clock, there was not a soul left in the city, except blind people and such as had had their noses or arms cut off, for he was very cruel. If one of his people committed any offence, he used to put out his eyes, or cut off his nose or an arm. We took these to our camp, and found our folks uninjured and

---

*Cf. Wissmann, I Afrika: Schilderungen und Ratschläge.' Berlin, 1895. Pp. 19 *et seq.*

in good condition, goods and all. Thereupon we went back to the city.

'Towards evening the enemy came in bands and surrounded the city. Some said, "We will break in in the night and slay them"; others, "We will try to break in towards morning." They had come in great masses, even the Sultan's sons, who lived at some distance-all had come except those who lived very far off. But I was wounded by the arrows which had struck me. I called Bushir bin Hahib el Wardi, my uncle, and said to him: "What do you think about it? Choose out the best men who are not afraid." And he got together some fifty or sixty of the best guns, and gave the men coarse shot, and they loaded the guns with shot and bullets. But the others, when they saw themselves so strong, and found that we were only few men, took courage: they lighted fires, and beat their drum, and smoked hemp and tobacco. Then I and Bushir bin Habib gave orders, and said to them: "Ten guns are to go to each door, for they will not see us because of their fire. Then shoot, and when you have fired off your guns come back." And they went, ten guns to the appointed door. When they came near the guns crackled, and on every side they fired off their charge at once, so that the Shensis said: "Perhaps they have pulled down the *boma*." Then the men came back. Suddenly we heard the Shensis calling to each other, then they lay down where they stood.

'The next morning, about a quarter to seven, our men went out, and saw that about 600 Shensis had fallen, and the weapons-spears, arrows, bows, drums, and axes-which they had thrown away were not to be counted. They had stood in groups, you see. We waited a short time. When it was two o'clock the Shensis advanced on us in great crowds. However, they were already frightened. We let them come close to the *boma*, then our people charged; and not seven minutes bad passed when they took to flight, and 150 men had fallen, while we had been lucky-only two men fell. And they were pursued for over two hours, then our people came back. Finally, on the third day even more of them came than on any of the previous days, and they came quite close to the *boma*. Our people charged, and routed the enemy, over 250 of whom were killed, and they were pursued a long distance. Not till seven hours afterwards did our men come back. On our side only three men were killed and four wounded.

'After that day they did not come back again, and there was no one there who claimed the ivory in the town. And we were in fear, for the country was large and the inhabitants many. And from the capital it was a quick four days' march with loads to Urungu, by the way we had come. And we remained in the city, in great fear, until I had recovered from those arrow wounds. When I was well I called together my men, freeborn and slaves, and said to them: What do you advise me to do?" But no one answered me. Then I said to them: "I have decided to march out and look for them, for for many days we have not known where they lie."

'Then spoke Bushir bin Habib el Wardi: "I will go; it is not good for you to march, for you are not strong enough yet." And he left twenty guns behind; he set off with all the rest. Even the people that had no guns-some 500 men-he took with him. About seven o'clock they started, and we waited till about five o'clock, when they had not yet come back, nor had we heard anything of them. And we were greatly afraid. At last, towards sunset, we heard the *ngoma* sound from beyond the mountain, and they fired guns, and gave vent to a shout of joy. Then they came themselves.'

They brought rich booty with them, some 1,000 slaves, and an untold number of goats. To be sure, a drop of gall was mingled with the rejoicing. On the march towards the frontier they had seen the corpses of many men of the coast that were unknown to them. As it afterwards turned out, a great caravan from Urungu had come into Nsama's country to buy ivory by the same route by which Tippu Tip had marched. They came to the country just when Nsama was defeated. Out of revenge, the strangers, who no doubt were believed to be in league with Tippu Tip, were attacked and cut down to the last man. The whole of their merchandise fell a prey to the Shensis. Tippu Tip now waited a few days more. But as nothing further was heard of the enemy, he was able to give himself up to the pleasant conviction that he remained the final victor.

The first thing was to secure the booty. Of ivory alone there appeared to be 1,950 *frasilas*, which, taking the *frasila* at the then price of £7, gave a profit of £13,650. At the present day, when a *frasila* costs about £15, the ivory taken would produce, in round numbers, £30,000-a small fortune. In addition to this, they took 700 *frasilas* of copper and a quantity of salt.

With these spoils Tippu Tip returned to Urungu. He was greatly honoured by the Sultan there, Chungu, for Chungu had long been an enemy of Nsama, at whose tardy fall he was naturally delighted. He at once offered to support the Arabs in further warfare against Nsama. With his help a deliberate war of extermination was carried on against Itahua, which, after two months, ended in Nsama's entire overthrow. He was granted peace in return for the payment of a large tribute. In these conflicts Tippu Tip, who was still suffering from the effects of his wounds, did not take part, but remained at Urungu.

Here he also met the English missionary Livingstone, to whose accounts we owe much concerning these regions and the events of that time. Although they are written in primitive fashion-the explorer, who was devoid of all proper means, at times used the edgings of newspaper sheets and ink from a tree for his jottings-yet, however fragmentary they may be, they are certainly accurate, and often more reliable than the reports of Tippu Tip, which were mostly somewhat boastfully compiled. Moreover, the Arab never makes a good historian. Whoever reads our hero's autobiography will feel that he suffers from the same prolixity as the chronicles cited at the outset of the oldest African history. Livingstone was then on his last journey, which he began in the early part of 1866 from Zanzibar, and on which, in April, 1873, he died in the village of Itala. He had marched up the Rowuma to the Nyasa, and had passed through the same districts as Tippu Tip. He made the, to us, interesting discovery that the Arabs had only penetrated to Urungu a very short time before. The older natives still very well remember the time when there were no Moslems in the country, and as yet the Moslem faith had not spread far.

On May 12, 1867, he heard that the Arabs had come to blows with Nsama. Accounts varied as to the reason for the quarrel, and it was difficult to get to the bottom of the matter. The friendly Arabs Said bin Ali bin Mansur and Thani bin Swelim recounted that Nsama's people had gathered in threatening fashion round the Arabs, who in their alarm fired, whereupon Nsama fled and left the assailants behind in the village. Others declared that a dispute had arisen about an elephant's tusk. Both accounts can be reconciled with Tippu Tip's statement as to the origin of the quarrel. But Livingstone's reports as to the issue of the conflict differ. According to him, the Arabs were by no means sure of success; they daily practised sorceries to discover how the further conflict with Nsama would turn out. So, too, the accounts of the booty obtained must have been exaggerated, for Livingstone received the impression that Tippu Tip had lost greatly by the Nsama expedition. The Arabs themselves confess to having lost fifty men against him. Nsama seems to have lost only a few more. According to his accounts, too, the Arabs had only 20 guns at their disposal, while Tippu Tip speaks of 105. Certainly the Livingstone's version would redound more to his credit, for the English explorer characterizes Nsama as the Napoleon of those regions.

On July 29 the two travellers met at Ponda, a village three days' journey from Lake Mueru. According to his journal, Tippu Tip presented Livingstone with a goat, a piece of white cotton, four large bushels of beads, and a bag of *sorghum*, and begged him to excuse his not being able to give more. Livingstone also records that Tippu Tip had received two wounds in the fighting with Nsama.

From Livingstone is very concise notes of the meeting with Tippu Tip we gather thus much-that the latter met him in a very friendly spirit. The Arab traveller's description of the meeting is still more in his favour. It appears that he found Livingstone destitute of all supplies. He describes him as quite an old man, and adds that his name was Livingstone, but that in the interior he called himself David. As an Arab, of course, he did not know the difference between Christian name and surname, and therefore regarded the two words as different names, just as he and his companions had their nicknames in the interior. Livingstone thus seems, like some other Europeans nowadays, to have been obliged, for the sake of greater intimacy, to have himself called simply by his Christian name by his blacks. This may bring the European humanly nearer to his inferiors, but in most cases undermines his authority. The black wants to feel a master over him; he has no respect for a brother.

According to his descriptions, Tippu Tip all but saved Livingstone from destruction. He supplied him for several days, conducted him to Lake Mueru, and later on sent him with letters of recommendation to Runda to his friend Mohammed bin Saleh, an old Arab, who then took him in hand. Tippu Tip also declared that he received various chests from Livingstone, together with a request to send them to Ujiji for him; these he at once forwarded on an opportunity happening to present itself, and that at his own expense. How far these statements are founded on fact cannot be estimated. On the one hand, the events lie so far back that a mistake of Tippu Tip's, who simply relates from memory, is not impossible; on the other hand, Tippu Tip, who always likes to play the *grand seigneur*, constantly distinguished himself by chivalrous hospitality. Livingstone, for his part, cannot withhold his approval from the Arabs in those parts; he finds them differing very advantageously from the slave-hunters whom he was accustomed to encounter in Ngao.

In addition to this, Tippu Tip always felt himself attracted to Europeans. At a very early date he became convinced of the essential inferiority of his fellow-tribesmen, and may have divined even then that the Europeans were a superior breed, with whom would rest the ultimate victory over those who had hitherto been the rulers of the country. In

Zanzibar Europeans had long been settled, who had traversed the broad seas and provided Moslem countries with treasures of civilization hitherto undreamt of by the Oriental. And that political power was combined with this wealth was proved by the warships of the Christians, which from time to time appeared in African waters, and had a wholly different aspect from the vessels of their Sultan, which seemed so powerful to the Zanzibaris. And though the English missionary whom the Arab traveller met here in the interior presented such a modest and even wretched appearance, yet the Oriental bowed before the spirit of enterprise which drove forth the man of the West to pursue with the simplest means ideals unknown to him, yet assuredly not worthless. What at that time, perhaps, was half instinct became later firm conviction in Tippu Tip, and, like a born diplomat, he always sided with the Europeans, even against his own countrymen, as soon as it seemed advantageous to him. His later history will furnish several further instances of this.

It is thus not improbable that events may have actually passed as Tippu Tip relates them. That Livingstone is silent about many occurrences proves nothing in view of the nature of his accounts, which are only quite short entries in a diary, made under the most difficult circumstances. On September 9 he had an interview with Nsama, whom he visited in his new *boma*, built close beside the old. He depicts him as an old man with a good head and face. As he could no longer walk, his people had to carry him. His belly was greatly swollen from much drinking of pombe. He showed himself very friendly towards Livingstone as soon as he had assured himself of his peaceful intentions, and promised to furnish him with guides for subsequent journeys in his territory. The negotiations, however, led to no result, as they were constantly interrupted by Nsama's people, who bore themselves very disrespectfully towards their ruler. Nsama seems really to have been very much given to alcohol, for a month later-October 18-Livingstone writes in his diary that the last he had heard of him was that he, a man of eighty, was performing dances to a musical accompaniment played by two women, and so would appear to have fallen into his dotage. In reality, however, it seems to have been only a question of a passing attack of drunken madness, for the Arabs maintained friendly relations with him for a long time afterwards. Only with his conqueror, Tippu Tip, Nsama would have nothing more to do.

It must also be mentioned that it was in these struggles that our hero received his well-known name. He himself declares that the Shensis, unaccustomed to the firing of guns, called him so because his muskets always went 'tip, tip.' Livingstone writes, on the other hand, that the sheikh, at the sight of Nsama's treasures, exclaimed: 'Now I am Tippu Tip, the gatherer of wealth.' If so, the etymology of the word remains obscure, for neither in Arabic nor in Swahili have the words the meaning attached to them by Livingstone. It can only be that a corresponding expression occurs in the Itahua language. Another version is also prevalent as to the origin of the name-viz., that Hamed bin Mohammed was so called on account of his nervous twitching of the eye, which must at once strike the African, who is particularly observant of bodily defects. In view of the fondness of the Swahilis for word-painting, this explanation seems quite intelligible. The first version is, of course, more agreeable to him.

Soon after the conclusion of peace Tippu Tip began his march back to the coast. He took his way through Urungu to Mambwe, and from there turned aside to Ruemba to fetch his brother Mohammed, whom he had left there. The inhabitants of the countries he passed through everywhere met him amicably. The news that he had beaten Nsama, who was reputed invincible, had spread with lightning rapidity in all the adjacent districts, and all exerted themselves to win the favour of the victor. Carriers placed themselves readily at his disposal to carry the captured treasures from place to place. After the return from Ruemba the march was at once continued to Unyamwanga, Ujika, and Usafa, until at last they arrived again at Urori.

Until then the inhabitants of the districts traversed had performed the duties of carriers, but now it proved impossible to obtain the requisite number of men for the further march to the coast. Tippu Tip therefore proceeded to Tabora to enlist carriers. When he arrived there he found the town deserted by the Arabs. His father, whom he would have liked to see again after years of separation, had gone on business to Kabwirr; his remaining compatriots had gone to war. Relations between them and Sultan Mkasiva were again strained.

Tippu Tip dismounted at his stepmother Karunde's, and was received by her with all honour. The only Arab remaining in Tabora, Suud bin Said el Maamri, brother of a rich merchant still living in Zanzibar, urged him to take up his abode with him, and only after a long competition between his two entertainers for Tippu Tip's coveted person, did the latter decide in favour of the more interesting company of his compatriot. Two days later the Arabs returned from their expedition. They had been beaten and had lost their leader. They were consequently in a very depressed state of mind. Tippu Tip quickly engaged the necessary carriers, and after waiting two months longer to no purpose for his father to come back, returned to Urori. Here a painful surprise awaited him. His confidential agent from Mbwa Maji had almost entirely made away with the merchandise entrusted to him to the value of 6,000 dollars; only two slave-girls were forthcoming, who had evidently pleased him and, as love is proverbially blind, had been bought by him at the unusual rate of 20 *frasilas* of ivory. To the experienced business eye of Tippu Tip this seemed unheard-of, and he angrily chained up the amorous youth. After four days he set him free again, philosophically remarking to himself: 'He who beats himself must not cry.' For that matter, things had gone no better with his brother Mohammed bin Masoud. His trusted agent had also made away with a considerable fortune, but managed to escape responsibility by falling ill of smallpox and dying.

After the pang of this unexpected loss had been got over the march to the coast began, the objective this time being Dar es Salaam. According to the custom still observed, the caravan spent the last night in the immediate neighbourhood of the town, so as to make its entry the next day quite fresh and in good order. On the 22nd day of Ramadhan, the sacred month of fasting of Islam, they had their last bivouac. At Dar es Salaam they found great changes.

Sultan Seyyid Majid, who with right judgment had realized that the basis of his power lay on the mainland which furnished him with his wealth, had determined to transfer his seat of government to Dar es Salaam, and already begun to build a palace worthy of himself there. Even before it was finished he spent yearly several months on the mainland, and the great importance attached by him to his plan is shown by the fact that he was staying there even in the month when the Arab usually retires into meditative seclusion, for he promised himself a great future for his rule from the place. True, he was unable to carry out his plans. A few years later he died suddenly, and with him vanished the interest in the further building up of the sovereignty on the mainland. The palace, whose erection he had so energetically begun, remained incomplete, like many private houses in Zanzibar started with insufficient means, and at last fell into a heap of ruins, the remains of which can still be traced near the hospital. If Majid had lived and been able to carry out his ambitious plans on the mainland, those daring expeditions of Dr. Peters and his companions to the Hinterland districts, which have led to the acquisition of a German colony in East Africa, would scarcely have been undertaken.

But for the time being things were lively at Dar es Salaam. All who belonged to 'society' had proceeded with the Sultan's Court to the new capital. All the non-trading Consuls and a great number of other Europeans, all the better-class Arabs from Zanzibar, Pemba, Mombasa, and Lamu, as well as a great body of Indians, had followed the Sovereign. Among the latter were all the creditors of Tippu Tip, in whom the arrival of the caravan naturally evoked great delight; for on seeing the rich spoil in ivory they felt certain of receiving back the money they had advanced with high interest. But beside this the coming of the caravan excited the greatest interest in all circles as being the first one bound for the coast to reach the new capital. The Sultan himself showed interest in the daring voyager, whom he loaded with high honours and entertained as his guest until the 'Great Feast,' which concludes the month of fasting (known in Turkey as the 'Festival of Bairam').

After the feast the whole Court returned to Zanzibar in three ships, headed by the Sultan and his notables and the foreign representatives on board a French man-of-war, while the remaining Arabs and the Indians followed in two smaller vessels.

CHAPTER IV

EXPERIENCES IN ZANZIBAR AND FRESH JOURNEY TO CENTRAL AFRICA

'Per angusta ad augusta.'

    At Zanzibar there set in for Tippu Tip, after his long years of wandering, a period of refreshment, which he could make as pleasant as he pleased now that he had grown rich in money and honours. But just as the European upon whom has once shone the tropical sun of Africa, like the moth that flies to the candle, ever feels drawn again to the land of palms, so the traveller who had grown used to life in the wilderness could not long endure the leisured repose of the city. After a few months he is again revolving fresh plans of travel, which are supported by the Sultan himself, who naturally would only be too glad if the distant interior were opened up as far as possible by Arabs. In the first place, it brought to the country rich produce in ivory and slaves, and then it increased the political influence of the Sultan that as many as possible of his subjects should achieve importance in the interior. He therefore offered Tippu Tip financial support as well, by directing the banyans who depended on him to give him credit up to any desired extent.

    'Banyan' is a generic name, under which in East Africa are classed all heathen Indians. They are divided into a great number of castes, of which the highest is that of the priests, or Brahmins. The other higher castes, of which especially the Batias and Wanyans are represented here, are all traders, and for the most part enjoy great prosperity, which it must be admitted they have not always earned in an irreproachable way. They are in part great usurers, and enrich themselves in that capacity by advances on land at high interest. But there are also very respectable banyans, who have earned their wealth in an honourable manner. For instance, the then head of the Batia community, Porsitom Tokarsi,* was highly respected among Europeans and natives. The Ivory King, Ratu Bimji, at Zanzibar, is also reputed a trustworthy man of business.

    Seyyid Majid had farmed the Customs to the then head of these banyans, one Ladda Damji. This man had grown most independent in his office and acted quite arbitrarily, as the Sultan did not trouble himself about internal affairs so long as he received his rent regularly. The farmer was, like his predecessor in the Gospel, a sinner. Among the Arabs whom he had managed to make dependent on him he was little loved. This Ladda,

---

*Since dead.

then-for so the Sultan desired-was to advance Tippu Tip the money for a new journey. The latter did not like this at all; he would much rather have borrowed of his former business friends, the Moslem Indians, but he did not dare to go counter to the will of the ruler, and so he agreed, submitting for the time with Oriental equanimity. After a time the Lord might yet order everything according to his desires.

So a year went by, till Tippu Tip was weary of inaction, and forged serious plans of travel. Heedless of his promise to Seyyid Majid, he turned to those who had previously given him credit, Nur Mohammed and Warsi Adwani, and declared to them he wanted to travel again, but was tired of borrowing, as before, of Tom and Harry. If they wanted to remain in commercial association with him, they must alone advance him the necessary goods. They replied that they could not supply all he wanted themselves, but that they would obtain what was wanted from Taria Topan (then an all-powerful Indian merchant, who later received an English title, and was called Sir Taria). On no account was he to have dealings with the banyan. But they delayed from day to day, while Ladda kept approaching Tippu Tip with fresh offers of credit. At last Tippu Tip entered into negotiations with him, and at once was assured of a credit of 50,000 dollars. Tippu Tip proudly remarks on this: 'And I had at that time not a plantation nor a house in Zanzibar or anywhere else in the world; but,' he adds, 'I had a wife in Zanzibar, Bint Satum bin Abdallah el Barwanie, who had much property in Zanzibar and Muscat.' The latter circumstance certainly did not weigh with the banyan, for he knew well enough that, in case things went wrong with Tippu Tip, she would not have come forward with a *pesa* to cover his losses. He must have reckoned on Kismet and Tippu Tip's star, and have also secretly cherished the hope that if he lost all his money, the Sultan, who had caused him to give the credit, would not leave him in the lurch.

So Tippu Tip went to the hated banyan, and received on the first day 6,000 dollars' worth of goods. When the carriers were going with them to his house, Warsi Adwani spied them out, and with all the jealousy of a rival at once asked for whom the things were. On their replying that they belonged to Tippu Tip, he rushed straight to Taria Topan to carry him the melancholy news. Taria was no less incensed, and called Tippu Tip to account, asking him how he could go to the banyans when he (Taria) had placed his whole credit at his disposal and commissioned Warsi Adwani to tell him so; he must just take the goods back to the banyan as speedily as possible.

This proposal, however, was more easily made than carried out. Ladda, of course, would not hear of taking the things back again. At last Tippu Tip had recourse to the plan of putting forward his relative Juma bin Sef bin Juma, who was to take the goods already delivered and some more as well. Tippu Tip, to be sure, had to be security for him with Ladda. Then Taria also hastened to deliver his supplies. It was the first time that he had lent on so insecure an enterprise as a caravan journey into the interior-a proof of how much confidence people placed in Tippu Tip's spirit of adventure.

Soon 200 loads were corded, which were sent on before to Ituru, the place of residence of old Mohammed. Tippu Tip himself still remained in the city, in order to procure the substance which would ensure the success of his journey-the indispensable gunpowder. This was before the Brussels agreement, and gunpowder was to be got easily and cheaply, 26 lbs. costing 4 dollars. He bought in round numbers 5,000 dollars' worth, or over 300 hundredweight! He unconcernedly stored it in his house, which stood in the midst of the European quarter, and left it there for ten days, until he could ship it in dhows to Bagamoyo. But this light-hearted carelessness was not to be without its sequel.

A month had passed since the shipment, when suddenly one evening two Arabs appeared at his house to summon him next morning before Sleman bin Ali, the Sultan's minister. With the cheerfulness of an easy conscience, our hero set off to see the dignitary, who asked him with an official air if it was he who had stored powder in the neighbourhood of the English Consulate. He calmly answered 'Yes'; which made the minister ask the further question whether Tippu Tip bad gone mad. 'No,' replied he; 'I am in full possession of my senses.' After this somewhat vague introduction the minister proceeded to deliver a long harangue as to its being quite illegal to bring powder into the city, and so endanger the lives and limbs of the inhabitants. Tippu Tip assured him he had had no idea of it; he had been years in the interior, and as a free man of course did not know the recent police regulations, but it should not happen again. But the minister was not content with this bill drawn on the future: ignorance of the law did not exempt from punishment; the offence had been committed and called for retribution, the more so that the English Consul had heard of the matter, and was very indignant about it; he was to come again next morning and hear the sentence that Seyyid Majid might pass on him.

When Tippu Tip appeared accordingly, he was informed that Seyyid Majid had not known that he was the transgressor, but that the matter had been mooted by the English Consul-General, and now he must either be locked up for a month or pay the price of the powder bought as a fine, Tippu Tip declared in favour of the latter. He estimated the value somewhat vaguely as more than 4,000 dollars, but he would rather pay the money than be confined even for a few days. Touched by such self-sacrifice, the minister advised him to allow himself to be locked up quietly for two or three days, and afterwards the matter would settle itself.

So Tippu Tip went to the prison, a solid foursquare building behind the toll-house, with a dirty courtyard in the middle and a tower at each of the corners, wrongly described as a Portuguese fort, though in reality it was only built at the beginning of last century by Seyyid Said. However, it was a cheerful prison for Tippu Tip. He was given a decent room, in which he could do as he pleased. During the day he received visitors, and at night his wives kept him company.

The conditions have even now not changed materially in this respect. A criminal who knows how to get on well with his custodians can still live pleasantly in Zanzibar Prison, if he does not prefer to open the door of his dungeon with a golden key.

When Tippu Tip was set free on the third day, he went to the English Consul-General, Sir John Kirk, who asked him where he had been hidden so long. He rejoined in dudgeon that he had been locked up on account of the powder. This was quite new to the Consul, who had indeed been angry about the business, but had no idea that Tippu Tip was the culprit. Otherwise-so Tippu Tip hints-he would have winked at the incident, for he valued him very much, since he had so chivalrously espoused the cause of the Consul's friend Livingstone, and had brought important letters from him to the Consulate.

Some weeks later Tippu Tip proceeded to Bagamoyo to despatch further loads to the interior. Even so goods to the amount of some 300 loads remained behind, which he requested Mohammed bin Masoud to make ready for conveyance. He himself wanted first to go once more to Dar-es-Salaam, to take leave of Seyyid Majid, who had returned there. As he also had to take leave of his business friends in Zanzibar, he instructed Mohammed to march on in the meantime, and expect him in a few days at Kwere, a place not far from Bagamoyo. His stay in Zanzibar, however, lasted longer than he anticipated, for he had to be present at a marriage there at the house of Rashid Adwani: both Oriental politeness and business considerations prevented his declining the invitation. Thus he was detained against his will seventeen days longer than he intended.

The consequence was that he found not a soul at Kwere. Mohammed had got tired of waiting, though he caught him up a few days later at Usagara, and from there they continued their journey together. But they had not got far up country towards Ugogo when a great disaster befell the caravan. Cholera broke out, and every day several carriers died. Moreover, the country presented many difficulties, for Ugogo was a poor district, in which provisions were scarcely to be had, especially as the population displayed hostility and nowhere offered anything for sale. 'Wherever we went,' complains Tippu Tip, 'we were driven back.' They had, it is true, to some extent supplied themselves at Usagara, but the provision taken with them was long since exhausted.

While in this unenviable plight they encountered on the highway one day, at the western limit of Ugogo, a body of armed warriors, who sought to bar their further progress. As disease was prevalent on the coast, the Shensis did not want to let the travellers pass through their townships, but urged them to march through the forest, and rejoin the caravan road again only at Mgunda Mkali, a steppe devoid of food or water and seven days' march in extent. The plan would have meant certain destruction, without provisions as they were and with the epidemic raging in the caravan. So a council of war was called. Tippu Tip requested his brother Mohammed, as the elder, to make the decision. But Mohammed bowed to Tippu Tip's greater insight, and left to him the decision, which was in favour of forcing a passage. When this was communicated to the soldiers they begged for a short respite, so that they might report to their Sultan Kiuje. Soon they came back, and announced that free transit was granted them, but they must encamp outside the first town on the river, and strike camp again after two days. Provisions would be brought into their camp. The river by which they took ground, however, was no river, at least for the time, for all the water was dried up; but by digging vigorously some springs were discovered, from which a scanty supply of water was obtained. Meanwhile the disease continued its ravages.

When the caravan, after the two days' rest, reached the western frontier of Ugogo by a longish march, it was already so thinned that there were not enough carriers left. A great number of loads were therefore buried-of course, only such goods as a lengthy stay in the ground would not hurt: beads, lead for the guns, chains, and so on. They then made their way through the desolate wilderness, by the Mgunda Mkali to Tura, where various Arab caravans were encountered which had started at the same time from Bagamoyo, but had taken another route.

These also had had dismal experiences. They had dwindled by a third through disease, and had in consequence of the loss of carriers also lost much merchandise. An acquaintance from Tabora also turned up here-the Arab Nasor bin Masoud-who had travelled to meet the much-damaged caravan of a business friend, in order to save as much of it as possible, as it had lost its leader through the epidemic.

At Rubuga, a further stage, Tippu Tip found his old father, who had marched to meet him, and awaited him here with the caravan that had gone on before. It was the first meeting between father and son after long years. Since the war with Mnywa Sere, at the close of which Tippu Tip had journeyed to Urua, they had not seen each other. 'At that time I was still a poor and unknown man, but many years have gone by since then,' says Tippu Tip in his autobiography, in proud recollection. Together they entered Tabora, where our hero naturally found many alterations.

A short time before his stepmother Karunde bad died, which caused the sorrowing widower, Mohammed bin Juma, at once to look about him for a new life-companion. There were enough aspirants forthcoming for the hand of the powerful chieftain, but he took into consideration only a daughter of Mkasiva, and Nyaso, a younger daughter of Fundi Kira. Mkasiva, who was very anxious to bind old Mohammed to him by the closest bands of relationship, left nothing untried to capture him as a son-in-law. But at last Nyaso gained the victory; and, writes Tippu Tip, just as had been the case with Karunde, so now again all the property, dead or alive, in Tabora was Mohammed's. But he had thus made an enemy of the ruler of the country-Mkasiva-as was soon to be seen.

An elephant was killed by Mohammed's men in the immediate neighbourhood of the town, whose tusks attained the splendid weight of $5\,^1/_4$ *frasilas*. Mkasiva, supported by the Vali Said bin Salum el Lemki, maintained that the ivory was his, as the elephant had been killed in his jurisdiction, and demanded its surrender. Mohammed and his wife Nyaso refused flatly, and now, after lengthy discussions, they were preparing to decide the point at issue by a regular war, when a more serious event suddenly reconciled the contending parties.

The Wangoni, a dreaded Wahehe tribe, threatened to invade the country. They had been called in by Mshama, a nephew of Mkasiva, who had himself aimed at the throne, and being, therefore, persecuted by his uncle, had fled to Uhehe, whence he was now returning, breathing vengeance. The enemy's hordes had already appeared in Njombo, a district some three hours south of Tabora. A force, hastily mustered from the people at Kwihara, was sent against them without delay, under the leadership of the Arab Abdallah bin Nasib, and the more distant Arabs, amongst them Tippu Tip, received a summons to assemble at once at Kwihara. From here they marched together after the advance guard, which they found in Njombo almost totally destroyed. They had been beaten by the Wangoni, and of the Swahilis alone had lost fifty, besides more than 100 Uganda men, who had happened to be at Kwihara and took part in the expedition. They had been sent by Sultan Mtesa to bring presents to Seyyid Majid, in return for the ample presents he had himself sent from Zanzibar.

After their victory over the Arab troops, the Wangoni, who probably cared less about the pretensions of Mshama to the throne than about making a profitable raid, had retired with large herds of cattle. Tippu Tip's proposal to follow on their heels found no response amid the general depression. All retreated hastily to Tabora. Here Tippu Tip once more unfolded his plans, and at length, on the second day, carried his point-in favour of immediate pursuit. The avenging force actually got as far as Msanga, in the immediate neighbourhood of Njombo, when the heroes again changed their minds and wheeled about towards their homes and Penates. Only Tippu Tip and another Arab named Said bin Habib continued the march. They advanced by Msuto, the western frontier place of Unyanyembe, as far as the river Njombo, which prevented any further pursuit. They saw that the Wangoni had already too long a start, and did not wish to expose themselves to the danger of encountering the enemy in a strange country, which, moreover, was divided from their home by a body of water that was difficult to pass. So they, too, returned to Tabora without having accomplished anything.

Tippu Tip did not wish to stay there any longer, but to go at once to Itahua, only the remaining Arabs would not let him. He must first wait and see that the Wangoni did not return to the attack. Now that they had gained an easy victory they would no doubt take a fancy to the business, and soon appear on a fresh raid. 'The folks were simply at that time not yet accustomed to war.'

Unwillingly Tippu Tip gave way. When two months of waiting had passed quietly away, he sent forward the greater part of his caravan to Itahua, and after another month a further instalment-all but a small portion, which remained behind under his own orders. Meanwhile, he had sent to Ugogo to have the buried goods fetched. They were fortunately found almost complete, except that a small portion of the beads had been lost in the sand. When they arrived, Tippu Tip got under way, in spite of the persuasions of his fellow-tribesmen, who would have liked to keep him with them for their own safety, and made his first halt in Ugalla, a district lying to the south-west.

CHAPTER V

FROM UGALLA TO THE KINGDOM OF LUNDA

'El ein bil ein wa 'I anf bil anf wa 'I udhn bil udhn wa's sin bis sin.' An eye for an eye, a nose for a nose, an ear for an ear, a tooth for a tooth.
KORAN: *Suret el Maide*, v. 45.

Ugalla was nominally ruled by a certain Taka as Sultan, in reality, however, by his younger brother Rijowe, who, according to Tippu Tip's descriptions, was a great tyrant and created all possible difficulties for travellers. He lived in a large town which was strongly fortified with ramparts and ditches. He allowed the caravan to pitch its camp outside the fortress at a distance of a quarter of an hour. Tippu Tip wanted to buy in his country sufficient provisions for eight days, which he required for his march to Ukonongo, but he did not obtain permission to do so until he had paid five oxen and a hundred garments. Thereupon he was allowed to make his purchases and handed over to his men their provisions in the shape of *mtama* (native corn), which they at once began to pound, partly in the camp, partly in the town itself. Unfortunately this corn was destined to be an apple of discord.

On the morning of the second day Tippu Tip was summoned to an audience with the Sultan. With a following of sixteen men, who as a precaution had with them guns loaded with ball, he went to the town. On the way he met one of his Swahilis, who told him furiously that a native had spilled all his corn and belaboured him with his fists; he was going now to fetch his gun and meant to avenge himself on the ruffian. Tippu Tip tried to induce him by persuasion to refrain from such disorderly methods, which would place them all in a most awkward position; it was a matter of importance to him to preserve peace, and he would gladly replace the spilled corn. Apparently satisfied, the young man withdrew, while Tippu Tip proceeded with his attendants to the Sultan's house. The latter greeted the strangers and conducted them to the dwelling of his principal wife, where they were to wait outside a few minutes. Meantime the injured Swahili came by, just as he had at first said, armed with his musket. Tippu Tip called him to him and dealt him several fatherly boxes on the ear-six or seven, so far as he remembers. But the chastisement came too late. The Shensis had already seen him and realized from the situation that he meant to be revenged on them. They raised a furious shout and charged in on Tippu Tip and his men. In the rain of spears and arrows a slave of Tippu Tip's fell.

Tippu Tip turned to the Sultan and called on him to control his subjects. But whether he felt himself powerless in face of the excited mob or was himself a party to the breach of the peace, he simply took to flight, but did not get far, being immediately brought down by a shot from the Arabs, who were now on their part using their weapons. At sight of their falling chieftain the natives took to flight.

But the Arabs, who remained on the spot, did not feel comfortable. The town was everywhere strongly fortified, and the concealed enemy might be lying in wait anywhere. They made in a body for the nearest gate-of which there were six-and returned to their camp outside the town. They found it quite deserted. Even the two sentries had disappeared. But as they stood between fear and hope at the main gate, which lay opposite their camp, a troop of people came suddenly towards them from within, headed by the red flag.* They had searched the town through and scarcely found a living soul. They brought with them only six women as prisoners of war.

Then Tippu Tip went back into the town to reconnoitre. It was quite deserted by the men, but sixty more women were found and welcomed as good booty. Also what merchandise and ivory they found-it was not much-was thankfully accepted. After Tippu Tip had become master of the field of battle he decided to camp inside the town, in order to secure himself against a more than probable attempt at revenge. He therefore summoned his people living outside in the villages by sound of drum, and in doing so again had the pleasant surprise of finding that a great portion of his brave fellows had vanished. No less than sixty Wanyamwezi were not forthcoming. If they had been killed their bodies would have been found; so it was quite clear that they had shown the white feather at the beginning of the fight. It was not far to their home at Tabora (five days' easy march without loads).

Under these circumstances it was not possible at once to continue the journey. Yet even if they decided to remain it was not easy to know what to do. Should they start in pursuit of the Shensis or remain idly sitting till they returned with reinforcements to attack them? Against the former the prudent Said bin Ali gave his voice; if the fighting men went out in pursuit the loads would still have to be left behind. Then how easily, when the Arabs had marched out, could the Shensis double back on the town another way and cut down the camp followers there!

So they stayed, and had not to wait long before the natives came back. On the eighth day, shortly before sunrise, when the Arabs were just at their first prayer, they heard the clamour of the advancing hordes. These were driven back with a few wellaimed volleys, and pursued for two hours. On the side of the Shensis some seventy men had fallen; the Arabs had only four killed and six wounded.

After eight days more they again heard the noise of an advancing host. The fear that it was a renewal of the attack was, however, not wellgrounded. They were men from Tabora, who had been sent by the Vali, at Seyyid Majid's instance, to Uganda. They brought with them letters from the Vali and old Mohammed containing favourable news. They had heard through the fugitive Wanyamwezi, who had in fact fled back to Tabora, of the

---

*In Africa every large caravan still bears the flag of its nationality. That of Zanzibar is blood red.

conflicts at Ugalla. Later on Sultan Rijowe had sought refuge with them, in order to obtain peace with Tippu Tip by their intercession. Now the Vali and Mohammed wanted to come themselves to set matters in the right channel. Four days later they came, and were received outside the town by Tippu Tip. But they would not make their entry until he had declared his readiness for the conclusion of peace. Tippu Tip agreed and accepted beforehand the conditions they might regard as right. After their entry they came to an agreement that Tippu Tip should give back the women he had taken, while the Shensis were only to pay compensation for those who had fallen on the side of the Arabs.

So peace was concluded. As the fugitive Wanyamwezi had come back with the Arabs from Tabora, there was nothing more to hinder the march. They moved via Ukonongo to Fipa, Sultan Karagwe's country. Here they rejoined their friends, who had gone on in advance, with Mohammed bin Masoud at their head. These had found the country, which enjoyed great fertility, so pleasant that they had decided to await the rearguard there. They had only sent on one of their number, Juma bin Seif bin Juma, to Itahua. Tippu Tip remained in Fipa six days, to provision his caravan in this fertile region for the impending march through more barren tracts; then they set off together-a column 4,000 strong. The way led along the shores of Lake Tanganyika, and presented many difficulties. The country there is very mountainous, and so they went up hill and down dale till at last they reached Urungu-an impoverished district, which they soon left again, as provisions were not to be had.

At last they reached the district of Itahua, and came to a town where Mkura, a son of Nsama, ruled. Here there was again great plenty, especially an astonishing crop of manioc, with which the famished carriers greedily repaid themselves for the privations of the past weeks. Some days later the whole band sickened with violent dysentery, to which forty men fell victim. Fortunately the Arab Juma bin Sef, who was trading in Itahua, appeared soon after with a remedy for the disease. He had a pungent curry sauce, stirred up with pepper and muscat, which he gave the men to eat with lean goat's flesh. This was given the patients for several days, and the homely remedy really had its effect. The dysentery gradually ceased, though the men were much exhausted for a long time after. The disease was not, however, as Juma taught them, caused solely by their voracity, but the manioc was of a different kind from what they had previously been accustomed to it was extraordinarily bitter, and only innocuous when it had been steeped for a considerable time in water, then allowed to dry for several days, and finally cooked. This Tippu Tip's men, of course, did not know, and even if they had known it they would probably not have observed the precaution, for in the eight days which they would have needed to make the manioc fit for use they would very likely have starved. They had not even taken the trouble to cook it, but consumed it raw, just as it came out of the ground.

When the caravan had recovered, they proceeded further to seek out their old acquaintance Nsama. To all the Arabs he gave a friendly reception, only he refused to see Tippu Tip. He sent, however, forty elephant's tusks, of a weight of 65 *frasilas*, as a present to his guest, but added that that was all the ivory he had. The assurance sounded scarcely credible, for shortly before he had sold to Juma bin Sef 300 *frasilas*, besides which the country swarmed with elephants. Tippu Tip's men employed themselves busily in hunting.

In particular, there were three of his slaves who distinguished themselves in woodcraft. He had bought them long before, almost against his will, from a bankrupt named Shihiri, who wanted money and offered him four men, the lot for 100 dollars (about 300 marks). One of them had escaped in Ugogo; the remainder now brought in their purchase-money, with interest. It was no rare occurrence for them to secure twenty tusks in one morning. There were also buffaloes in abundance, which were hunted for the sake of their meat.

As Tippu Tip could not hope for much from a further stay near his old enemy, he left his hunters behind and went on to Ruemba, where Sultans Mwamba, Kitimkaro, and Shanza ruled. For but a small amount of goods he obtained a great deal of ivory, wherefore he bears witness that they were good people. He returned once more with his treasures to Itahua, where he now concocted a fresh plan. Mohammed bin Masoud was to remain with the bulk of the merchandise in the country, while Tippu Tip purposed, taking all the beads that the two had with them, to proceed westwards to Urua, where beads were fetching high prices.

Their way led them through the once powerful and still very important Kasembe kingdom of Lunda, which at the end of the eighteenth century had been visited by Portuguese discoverers, and in 1866 and 1867 was systematically explored by Livingstone. It is a fertile plateau to the west of Lake Mueru, bounded on the north by Itahua and Kabwire, on the south and east by Lombemba and Kisinga. The country was governed by elected rulers called Kasembe, a word that, according to Livingstone, signifies 'general.' The Kasembes seem to have changed very often, as they were deposed as soon as they became unpopular. The ruler whom Livingstone found there in 1867 was called Maonga, and was the seventh Kasembe; but his predecessor, Lekwisa, was still alive, and in exile with Nsama. Livingstone visited Maonga on November 28, 1867, in his capital at the north end of Mofwe-a lake abounding in fish, formed by the Luapula above the larger and better known Mueru. Each Kasembe used to found a separate town as his Place of residence. The capital of the then reigning Kasembe covered an area of an English square mile, on which some hundreds of huts lay scattered among cassava plantations. The court of the ruler-many would have called it a palace-formed a quadrangle 300 ells in length and 200 in breadth, and was surrounded by a high bamboo hedge. Men's skulls were displayed here and there as a decoration. A great portion of the people had cropped ears and lopped-off arms-mutilation which were not inflicted on the subjects for aesthetic reasons, as in the case of fox-terriers with us, but only to furnish them with a life-long reminder that their ruler had once been obliged to give expression to his disapproval of their conduct.

The first impression was not by any means reassuring to the visitor, but he was soon compensated for the feeling of horror which came over him on entering by the amusing spectacle which presented itself as he went further. Before his hut, on a couch of lion and leopard skins, sat a figure with a squinting face, wrapped in a coarse garment of white and blue striped material, with a red border bunched out voluminously, so that he looked as if he had put on a crinoline the wrong way around. The arms, feet, and head were clad in sleeves, trousers, and cap, with a beautiful pattern of coloured beads, while this strange fashion-block was crowned with an aigrette of yellow feathers. The grandees of the kingdom, shaded by huge patched umbrellas, approached their master respectfully, bowing ceremoniously before him, and then took their places on his right. Livingstone was presented by a minister with cropped ears to the Kasembe, who, after being briefly informed as well as might be of the purpose and aim of the explorer's journey, was pleased to accept his presents. As they partly consisted of grotesque garments, he was highly delighted, which did not hinder him from requiting them with nothing but a lean goat and a few fish. At a subsequent audience he was openly mocked for his meanness by the Arab Mohammed bin Saleh, who had lived ten years in the country.

Livingstone has no high opinion of the power of the Kasembe of his day. He thinks if he had to summon the array for war, he would scarcely be able to get together 1,000 vagabonds, whereas the first Portuguese visitor, Pereira, records that the Kasembe he found there had a standing army of 20,000 trained warriors. Livingstone has the impression that he could have established friendly relations with Maonga, whom he lectured on the iniquity of the slave trade, only the sight of his squinting eyes and the many mutilated people always deterred him.

When Tippu Tip came into the country some years had passed since then, and another Kasembe was already on the throne. The entry into Lunda did not take the form of a welcome to him. Amid heavy rainstorms, which allowed the great caravan to progress but slowly, they reached the frontier of Itahua. On the way they had received the consoling intelligence that Nsama, after Tippu Tip's departure, had exhibited great stores of ivory, which he had been unwilling to show his conqueror, but which the Arabs now could purchase at their ease. The boundary between Itahua and Lunda was formed by a river, which, owing to the rainy season, was greatly swollen. The caravan had to march a great distance upstream before it could ford it. As the leading files reached the land they were attacked by the Walunda, who struck down four men and took a quantity of merchandise and muskets. As the Kasembe was at enmity with Nsama and had no reason for treating Tippu Tip, who was well enough known as an opponent of Nsama's, in an unfriendly way, this reception was most startling, and our traveller resolved, before retaliating, to inquire into the causes of this unexpected hostility. He was haughtily answered that the Walunda had attacked the Arabs' followers quite deliberately, for they had boasted that they had defeated Nsama, and now they, Kasembe's men, would show them they were something different, and had determined to strike down every intruder into their country. This impudent reply demanded immediate retribution. Even Said bin Ali el Hinawi was of this opinion—a *mutawa*,* a pious and forgiving man who had once stood in high honour in Zanzibar, but later, as an adherent of Bargash, fell into disfavour with Seyyid Majid, and when the latter so far humiliated him as to give him a box on the ears, retired in dudgeon and went on his travels. In spite of all, he had retained his pious disposition, and was always ready to give good advice when it was possible; but now even he advised fighting. More troops

---

* Literally, 'a very obedient.' The people are so called who devote themselves to a specially religious way of life. They wear as a badge the white turban, which many certainly assume without being entitled to do so; *e.g.* the well-known Wali Sleman bin Nasor always wears it, though, in view of his unprejudiced attitude towards the prohibition of winedrinking, he has no claim to the distinction.

were sent for in haste from Itahua; the river forming the frontier was crossed, and in a few months all Lunda was subjugated. The Kasembe-Tippu Tip did not remember his name-was driven from the country, and a new chief named Mabote set up in his place. This man had been Kasembe once before, but had been deposed by his people because he refused to submit to circumcision, which was not otherwise customary in the country, but was expected of its rulers.

CHAPTER VI

ENTRY INTO URUA

'Duobus certantibus gaudet tertius.'

After thus subduing the mighty kingdom of Lunda, they proceeded next in a northerly direction along Lake Mueru, until they reached the capital of Sultan Mpueto. Here the Congo issues from the lake under the name of Luapula. The river there is of course narrow, and was easily crossed in boats. On the left bank lay Urua, the objective of the travellers. At first not much was to be discovered of the much-boasted power of the country. The natives were weak in bodily structure, frequently disfigured by goitres, and immoderately addicted to the enjoyment of tobacco and hemp, a passion which procured them from their western neighbours, to whom smoking seemed contemptible, the nickname Wahemba: *watumwa vuaka-i.e.*, slaves of tobacco. As their country adjoined those of the marauding Nsama and Kasembe, they were, of course, exposed to constant unexpected attacks, and were thus rendered specially timid and suspicious. Moreover, the natural conformation of their territory tended to impose the defensive on them. The country was rich in caves, which ran far into the mountains and offered ample shelter to several hundred men. As they were stalactite formations, there was no want of water inside them. Provisions could be taken into them to any amount desired, and, when the times were warlike, were stored up there beforehand. Tippu Tip recounts his visit to such a cave, which had two entrances and at the largest point was some 12 feet wide. He went in with candles, but contented himself with examining the cavern. His uncle, Bushir bin Habib, had more pluck, and came out at the other end of the mountain, after a long progress through dark passages.

In case of war these caves, of course, afforded an excellent refuge. On the enemy's approach all the townships were deserted, and the inhabitants vanished from the soil. Later on Msire, Sultan of Katanga, which lay to the south-west, fathomed the secret, and, as later conquerors have dealt with similar troglodytes, smoked them out like a fox from his earth. He placed burning wood before one opening and let the smoke penetrate, until the caved-wellers came out on the other side and submitted.

On pursuing his march, Tippu Tip came upon a Sultan named Kajumbe. His subjects were stronger men than the Warua of the frontier, and he himself, who, on account of his imperiousness, bore the surname Kha Ukuma, the Swashbuckler, wielded considerable power, which he made the newcomers feel. For all the ivory which they purchased they had to pay a high duty, which was here called *kiremba*. At the same time, the yield of ivory of the country was slight and the natives hard to deal with. A bargain over a single tusk often lasted for several days.

Thus the news came most opportunely that in rather more distant regions far more favourable conditions of trade prevailed. Two Sultans, named Mrongo Tambwe and Mrongo Kassanga, sent messengers to Tippu Tip, who brought him several tusks as a present and said that in their country there was plenty of ivory; if that was what Tippu Tip wanted he had only to come to them. But they dared not bring it for exchange into Kajumbe's territory, for, warned by previous experiences, they feared that most of it would be stolen from them.

Even Msire, the great Sultan of Katanga, sent an embassy of homage with twelve elephant's tusks. He had heard that Tippu Tip had passed triumphantly through Nsama's and Kasembe's country, and was now afraid lest the mighty conqueror should make war against him too. Our traveller, who to be sure had as yet entertained no such thought, at once took advantage of this favourable frame of mind and sent an answer that such was certainly his intention, 'It is true, I have heard that he is a very bad man and attacks people without cause. If necessary, I will come and chastise him-unless he sends twenty more tusks beside these.'

Much alarmed by these haughty words, Msire's people departed, taking with them, if possible, a still higher opinion of the intruder than they had before.

To get away, to be sure, was not such a simple matter. Kasembe, in fact, cherished the opinion that travellers who came into his country were bound to dispose of all their goods there. How long they took about it did not matter to him if they only paid plenty of duty. Tippu Tip, however, did not feel disposed, with his rich supplies of beads, to wait there whole decades for ivory that might or might not come, and as peaceful negotiations were of no avail, he made his exit by force. After an hour's fighting the Warua took to flight, and the next morning Kajumbe sued for peace, which was granted him in return for nine elephant's tusks.

Three days later they came upon a Sultan named Mseka, in whose village a two days' halt was made. During this sojourn envoys came once more from Mrongo Tambwe, who sent presents of ivory and again invited the travellers to visit his country. Tippu Tip replied that it did not matter to him where he went if there was only ivory, and followed his emissaries.

After two days' march the guides halted at some cross-roads and announced that from there there were two ways: the one led through uninhabited, waterless jungle, but had the advantage of security; if they took the more convenient path through inhabited places, they would have to be constantly fighting. The position was as follows: the country for which they were making stretched alone Lake Kissale, a broad, swamp-like continuation of the Lualaba. This lake was the very life of the country. It was abundantly rich in fish, and yielded its inhabitants, without difficulty, ample sustenance. There were also endless swarms of wild ducks, which it was not difficult to bring down. Nay, this beneficent lake was made subservient even to elephant-hunting. The forests were beaten and the mighty pachyderms driven towards the water. There they lost themselves in the muddy, reed-grown banks, and the natives, hastening to the spot in boats, killed them with spears without difficulty.

No wonder, then, that rich settlements with a brisk traffic sprang up round this lake. People came from far and wide to barter for its products. In exchange for the fish, which, when dried, were exported long distances, they brought the produce of their own districts. The chief articles of barter were the so-called *viramba*, fabrics woven out of the bark of trees, such as are still often seen in East Africa, imported from Madagascar. These fabrics were then worn throughout Manyemaland, and had such a universally acknowledged value that they were regarded as a substitute for money. Another important article was a kind of tree-oil.

In this favoured country, once peacefully united under one sceptre, two near relatives had for many years been striving for the mastery, Mrongo Tambwe and Mrongo Kassanga. First one was victorious, then the other. The victor always took up his residence on the lake, while the conquered fled into the jungle until he was once more strong enough to attack and overcome his rival. The part of the conquered was being played just at that time by Tambwe, which was why he had been in such a hurry to secure the friendship of the newcomer.

To Tippu Tip it was of course a most welcome state of things that he could intervene in the internal affairs of the country with a certain show of right, and it was especially to his advantage that, since the two rivals were about equally strong, he must, by interposing with his seasoned troops, splendidly armed as compared with the natives, infallibly decide the matter. He therefore had not the slightest intention of acting on the proposal of the Warua guides, and stealing by the forest route to Tambwe. But as the Warua did not dare to follow him on the way through the towns, he took only two of them with him as guides, but dressed them up, for the sake of their peace of mind, in Swahili clothes, so that they might not be recognised by their enemies.

They at once entered fertile, richly populated districts, in which one township succeeded another. They pitched their camp in a town five hours' march from the lake. Mrongo Kassanga, who was himself sojourning on the lake, sent envoys to them, asking them to pay him a visit the next day. The answer was they were on the way to Mrongo Tambwe, and had nothing to do with him. 'Yes,' answered Kassanga's men, 'he was somewhere in the wilderness, and had been driven out by them. If they insisted on going to their enemy, they would be attacked and overcome.' Nor were hostilities long in ensuing. In the afternoon some members of the caravan were attacked while fetching water, and their utensils stolen. Tippu Tip, who was eager to attack at once, allowed himself to be persuaded by the milder Said bin Ali to keep the peace for the time. He decided to demand an explanation from Mrongo Kassanga next morning.

In the night, however, it was clear that the natives were planning war. All round drums sounded, which, as the Warua they had with them recognised from the sound, were summoning the people to battle. When the caravan was getting under way next morning it was attacked. The onslaught, however, was successfully repulsed. Some townships were set on fire, and several hundred prisoners taken.

Next morning, quite early, the drums again sounded. The Arabs were afraid that this meant a fresh attack, but their guides assured them that these were the drums of Mrongo

Tambwe's followers. Presently 500 men arrived, and brought the news that their master was just making his entry into the townships on the lake, and begged his Arab friends to meet him in the capital. When, after a fair fight, it was again Tambwe's turn, the natives were soon on the scene again, and commerce flourished as in the days of his exiled rival. The new Sultan showed himself very friendly towards his foreign allies. In particular he sent them daily boatloads of fish.

However pleasant life on the lake might be, it did not offer what the travellers sought first and foremost. There was much less ivory here than even in Kajumbe's territory. Then Tippu Tip heard that there was probably a great deal in a country called Irande. The news was indeed not fully vouched for, for other informants reported, on the contrary, that there was no trade there in ivory-only in fabrics made of tree-bark. Tippu Tip said to himself, however, that a country into which no freeborn man had penetrated since the Creation must certainly harbour ivory, and set off.

Shortly before their departure emissaries again came from Msire to entice the travellers into his country. To the inquiry about what objects of barter were most attractive there, they replied that European fabrics were in request. As Tippu Tip had only beads with him, Said bin Ali was told off for the journey to Katanga. He had at the time been unable to make up his mind, like the other Arabs, to leave his fabrics behind in Nsama's country, and now hoped to make his fortune out of the loads that had been so long dragged with him for nothing. As soon as his trading was concluded, he was to return to the Arabs who had remained at Itahua.

So Said proceeded southwards, protected by thirty muskets. Tippu Tip advanced further into the unknown west. Guided by some men of Mrongo Tambwe's, he crossed the Lualaba, but soon turned back when he heard that an acquaintance of his-Juma bin Salum-was staying in the neighbourhood near the capital of a chief named Kirua. This Arab, generally known by the sobriquet of Juma Mericano,* and so styled in many books of travel by European explorers, was one of the oldest traders in the interior of Africa. As early as 1858 Burton and Speke, the daring discoverers of Lake Tanganyika, had come across him at Ujiji. He had since then carried on trade uninterruptedly in Itahua, Lunda, and Katanga, and since the early seventies had kept a standing camp near Kirua on Lake Usenge. The traveller Cameron found him in October, 1874-somewhat later than the occurrences here described-at his fortified settlement, Kilemba, in Kassanga's country, and describes him as a 'handsome, dignified man,' and the most amiable and hospitable of the Arab traders in Africa with whom he came in close contact.

Tippu Tip endeavoured to get his friend to accompany him on his journey to Irande, but met with no response. Juma Mericano took the position that a certain profit on a small scale was preferable to the uncertain expectation of great wealth, and crowned his objections by declaring that he could not enter a country in which no Arab had yet set foot. Tippu Tip called him a coward and started off alone. The ivory he had so far acquired-300

---

* Mericano was originally a cotton material imported only from America. Juma was so called because he dealt principally in it.

frasilas-he left behind.

On entering Irande there was at first not much sign of ivory, but, on the other hand, the country offered all the more interest in other respects. As to the impressions he received there and the occurrences that ensued, we will let him give his own account in the next chapter.

Native man

CHAPTER VII

THE NEW SULTAN OF UTETERA

'May one deceive the people ?
I say not so.
Yet if you must delude them,
Be it not too subtly done.'
GOETHE: *Epigrams.*

'The towns of the country were astonishingly large and their number boundless. Their business is to weave *viramba*. They build their towns in such a way that there is a row of houses here and another row there, like the rows of clove-trees. In the middle there remains a vacant space, which is some 40 ells wide, or perhaps more, and the number of the houses is fifty here and fifty there. In the middle they build a remarkably big house with a *baraza*, in which all the craftsmen assemble to weave *viramba*. One may walk in a town for six, seven, or eight hours. All their towns are built in the same way: a row of houses here, and another row there, and in the middle the work *baraza*. So we marched about the land of Irande, and however long we waited and inquired for trade in ivory, there was nothing but *viramba*. And in this country they knew nothing of freeborn men, nor at that time did they know of guns. The Warua went into this country and brought fish there to purchase *viramba*, and if they saw ivory they at once obtained it at a low price; only there was no ivory. And the Warua had no guns; they had only bows and arrows as weapons; guns they did not know. They asked if the guns we had were *mituwangu*, which means "rammers." We said, "Yes," and they thought they were rammers. So we journeyed until we came to Sultan Rumba. There was no ivory; their trade was just this *viramba*. And every town was enormously big; every town was a whole country. So we passed through ever so many districts till we came to Sultan Sangwa, at Mkasuma; only there he is called Mfisonge.

'There are no native Sultans in these countries, but people come there from far away, who give goods and make payments to those who own the lands; and these set up such a one as Sultan for a period of two years. As soon as one has established himself, another comes from far off in the same way, builds himself a house in the forest, and pays goods, stuffs, slaves, goats, beads, and vegetable oil until he who reigned before him has finished his two years and retires. Then the other steps in-such is the custom there-and receives the produce of two years. And likewise in those regions, when anyone dies who is in debt and cannot pay, they do not bury him; or if he is buried, those who have buried him must pay.

He is taken into the forest, and they hang him upon the fork of a tree. Below they place his hoe or his axe or a basket at the place where the dead man is hung up. If anyone comes who has a claim on him, he is told: "If you will have what is yours from yonder debtor, take his axe or his hoe." Such is the nature of their laws and customs.

'And as we marched they committed many acts of violence against us and robbed us; but we put up with it, for they acted as if we had no weapons, as if we carried rammers. So we marched until one day we found a Shensi who could speak Kirua tolerably. He asked us: "What is really your desire?" We answered him: "We are looking for ivory." Then he said: "If you want ivory, cross the Lomami, and go to Koto; there is much ivory there. Or go to Utetera, to Sultan Kassongo Rushie, the son of Mapunga. That is not at all far from here. There is plenty of ivory there. This Kassongo Rushie is very old, and had two sisters, named Kina Daramumba and Kitoto. And a long time ago, as we have heard from our parents, there was a great Sultan in Urua named Kumambe. His second name was Rungu Kabare. He was very powerful, and ruled all Urua as far as Mtoa, and he made war upon all the Manyema lands and the lands on the far side of the Lomami. He came also to Utetera, and carried off the two sisters, Kina Daramumba and Kitoto. They are of the race of the Wana wa Mapunga. There there is very much ivory. And two roads lead there. One passes through Nsara, and the Sultan is called after the country, Mwinyi Nsara. By this road you will come across Kasongo Rushie, who is on good terms with the people of Nsara. On the second road you will come to Mkahuja. The people there are among the opponents of Kassongo Rushie-the people from Nsara and Nguo and Kibumbe and Isiwa, and Mkatwa and Msangwe-in short, more than twenty countries with great Sultans, not counting a number of small Sultans-all these have banded themselves together to fight against Utetera. And the inhabitants of Utetera are very numerous, but rather stupid. When they are attacked they become terrified. Every time they were attacked they were beaten, and that has made them still more cowardly." I wrote down all the stories which that Shensi told me.

'We went on and marched until we came to a place where we saw that our people had halted; the road branched off there. And they asked us: "Where do you want to go?" We said to them: "We are going to Kassongo Rushie at Utetera." They replied: "That is this way-take it!" We marched further and bivouacked in villages. In the morning we started off again. When it was twelve o'clock we came to towns of another kind. The inhabited places succeeded one another; they were not built like those we had come from. They were built as in Urua-large towns and many in number. One could see how one town joined another, for the country is very open. We remained twelve days, and it rained during that time. They brought us very much ivory, and it was cheap. For two *vivangwa* and a red coral and a garment you got 2 or 3 *frasilas* of ivory. The tusks had no value. You gave as much as you wanted to give and then said: "Off with you quickly!" When twelve days were past ivory became scarce. Then came a Shensi who could speak Kirua very well. He was a great rogue, and was called Pange Bondo. He brought about four tusks and begged for my friendship. I said: "Well, you are my friend." Then he said to me: "I have been Sultan in this country, and we have the following rule: Out of those who are born in the sovereignty one line always comes to power. When one line retires the other takes its place-and so on, each line in its turn. Each remains in power for two or three years, and then withdraws without contention. Then another succeeds." Pange Bondo, however, refused to retire when his time was out, and they made war, and the Sultan whose turn it was next was beaten. They deposed him and chose another Sultan. And they said to him: "You will not get the sovereignty again, even when the Sultans who now precede you have finished their time, nor will your children ever succeed, for you have offended against our Constitution." Then he knew he would not rule again. When it came to his turn another succeeded to the throne.

'When we saw that trade fell off and no more ivory was forthcoming, we decided to go to Utetera. The Shensis of Mkahuja said to us: "You must not go to Utetera before having been to Kirembwe." In the morning we started and proceeded to the frontier of Mkahuja. When we reached that frontier the Sultan came in the afternoon with about 400 men. They asked us: "Where are you going?" I answered them: "To Utetera." Then the Sultan said: "Give me presents, then we will grant you permission." We gave him some twenty garments and ten garments to his men and about 2 *frasilas* of beads. He said: "It is well." Just then people came from Kirembwe and said to us: "You must come to Kirembwe; you must not go to Utetera. The Watetera, you know, are subject to us; we have often marched out and defeated them. But now we will fight against them, you and we, and the ivory we will give to you; the women we will take ourselves." But we said to them: "We will only go to Kassongo at Utetera." We waited till the afternoon, then four Shensis arrived, who came from Utetera; they had marched through the forest and came to our camping-place. They asked: "Where is Tippu Tip?" Then they were brought to me, and I asked them: "What do you want?" They replied: "Kassongo Rushie sends us. He begs that you will come to him. There is much ivory there; what you have bought comes from us." Then I said to them: "It is well. Utetera, you must know, is my home. Kassongo is my grandfather."* They asked: "How so?" I told them: "Ages ago there was in Urua a Sultan, Rungu Kabare Kumambe, who made war on all countries, and amongst others came against Utetera. There he took captive two women, Kina Daramumba and Kitoto, and took them with him to Urua. There my grandfather, Habib bin Bushir el Wardi, my mother's father, who had also come to Urua, met them, and he bought one of the women and made her his wife. In this way my mother was born. When I was born she said to me: "In my own country I am a great Princess, and there is very much ivory there. And our elder brother is called Kassongo Rushie Mwana Mapunga.' Then I decided to come, and fought with everyone who came in my way, with the object of reaching my home." These men were seven in number: four left us on the spot and three remained with us in fear, and we concealed them. In the night the drum was beaten, and the Shensis said: "To-morrow there will be war."

'In the morning came that Sultan of Mkahuja with 400 of his people. The place where we had made our camp was surrounded by towns; they were all large places. We had all of us slung our guns about us, and had small shot and bullets ready. Then two tusks

---

* Properly 'great-uncle.' The Swahili always has at his disposal a great number of babas, mamas, and babus.

of ivory were brought us while we were engaged in fastening up our loads and packing our tents. The tribesmen who were with me said: "You go on with the guns; we who are behind will conclude the bargain." But I said to them: "That will not do; these Shensis have been beating the war-drum all night, and the people we have with us, the Watetera, say that we shall quite certainly be attacked, and the principal chief of Kirembwe, named Kingoigoi, has barred our way; therefore, it is better to conclude the bargain while we are all together." So we proceeded to conclude the bargain, and while doing so we were surrounded by a great crowd of Shensis; the Sultan and his people were in the middle of it. But we had said to our men: "No guns are to be fired unless someone is attacked, for these people believe our guns to be rammers; it is better that they should continue to think so." Suddenly we heard the report of two guns, and at the same time came two of our Wanyamwezi who had been hit by arrows. Directly afterwards we saw the Shensis flinging spears at us. Then we attacked them.'

Of course it was an easy matter to defeat their wholly untrained hordes. As usual, several towns were burnt down, and the inhabitants with their cattle driven off. Their simplicity showed itself afresh in their begging Tippu to recall their fallen countrymen to life. The report of the guns, which they thought *muhogo* - crushers, seemed to them thunder. As storms were very common in their country, they believed that their fallen brethren had fainted at the sudden claps, and would easily be waked again with a little *dawa* (magic drugs).

Peace was negotiated by Pange Bondo, Who stipulated as a main condition that he should be again set up as Sultan. This was willingly granted him by Tippu, but the Mkahuja people, as a counterpoise, demanded their captured fellow-tribesmen back. To this, too, Tippu agreed at the advice of his friend, for most of the captives were, as was proved later, not children of the country, but slaves from Utetera. After the conditions had thus been agreed to, Pange Bondo was restored to his old inheritance with great pomp. The coronation was performed in this way: his subjects clapped moist clay on his head and strewed flour over it; round his neck they hung a chain and ten living chickens. This ornament he had to wear for ten days, without regard to the fact that the birds died off in the meantime. On the handing over of the prisoners the wily Pange once more showed himself a true friend to Tippu. The latter naturally did not possess ethnological experience enough to distinguish the people of Mkahuja from the Utetera prisoners, and without the help of the new Sultan would have been badly overreached.

With the mocking humour peculiar to him, the autobiographer recounts in a graphic way how Pange helped him out of his difficulty. One morning the two augurs, followed by a crowd of people, proceeded to a large vacant space where the prisoners of war were marshalled. Tippu Tip seated himself and took a book in his hand, from the magic formulae of which, as he informed the wondering assemblage, he would learn which of the prisoners was a native of the country and which a Mtetera.* He made the men march past

---

* The prefix *u* signifies the country, the prefix *m* (plural *wa*) its inhabitants; *ki* at the beginning of a word signifies language, custom, quality.

singly, and with confounding accuracy pronounced the first dozen to be Watetera; the thirteenth was the first of Mkahuja's men. And so it went on, until it turned out that, out of a thousand prisoners, only about a hundred were fellow-tribesmen, who were given back, according to the agreement. The crowd was speechless with consternation at the omniscient stranger, and Pange himself, the old rascal, affected boundless astonishment. He jumped about as if possessed, slapped his legs with his fists, and cried: 'Just look at the sorcerer! You wanted to fight with a man like that!'

The solution of the riddle was very simple. It had been agreed that Pange should make him a sign every time a fresh prisoner was marched by. If he cast down his eyes, it was a Mtetera passing; if the passer was a man of Mkahuja, the chief looked up in the air.

The caravan got under way with its new booty, and after four days' march reached a town called Msange, on the borders of Utetera. The name Msange signifies, in the author's opinion, a settlement of men belonging to various tribes who had joined together here on the frontier to keep off common enemies. It was thus not a wholly Watetera town, though these seemed to form the majority.

After the travellers had made themselves at home on the camping-ground assigned to them, a relative of the Sultan, named Ribwe, visited them, who struck Tippu Tip by his exceptionally large build. To him Tippu Tip again dished up his well-prepared tissue of lies as to his relationship with the Sultan, and recounted in a touching way how year by year, not shrinking from war or privations, he had journeyed in order to see the relatives of his much-loved mother.

Ribwe, whom the vast knowledge of the stranger must have fully convinced, was so touched by this proof of his kinsman's affection that he at once sent his new cousin 300 goats and 20 elephants' tusks, and informed the Sultan, who lived four marches away, of the joyful discovery. Kassongo, equally convinced, at once sent envoys to fetch Tippu Tip. He did not require much pressing, and hastened to the capital, which was of moderate size, and inhabited only by Kassongo and his wives; it was, however, completely surrounded by larger towns. Kassongo himself, the ruler of an important tract between Lomami and Sankurru, was an old man of eccentric habits. The only beings that he regarded as his social equals were the sun and the elephant. He considered both these as Sultans like himself. He demonstrated his respect for the sun by never looking at the sunrise or the sunset, for he considered it improper to watch the toilet of his royal brother. His regard for his brothers the elephants he displayed by never eating their flesh or touching their tusks.

If one may believe Tippu Tip, Kassongo voluntarily resigned the sovereignty over the whole country in his favour the very morning after his arrival. Extraordinary as this may seem, yet it appears to have been the truth that our traveller with his clumsy artifice found credence, and at once became ruler of the country. To the simple Shensis, who till then had scarcely come into contact with civilized tribes, it must have seemed inexplicable how a stranger come from afar should on his first entry into the country be acquainted with the whole genealogy of the Sultan's family. Moreover, it stood Tippu Tip in very good stead that he had had the opportunity at Mkahuja of making prisoners of several hundreds of Watetera. These he brought back to his adopted grandfather as a present, and was thus enabled to show his family feelings in a most disinterested fashion, and so destroy any possible doubt of the genuineness of his blood-relationship. So he became Sultan of Utetera, in full legal sovereignty. He exercised justice and exacted heavy penalties from all who committed offences. He also appointed subordinate rulers, who had to pay him heavy tributes. Kassongo's conscientious attitude towards the elephants turned particularly to his advantage. As the succession in the office of ruler did not bind him to share the scruples of his kinsman, he could take all the ivory for himself, and if he does not exaggerate, within a fortnight he had acquired 200 tusks, of a weight of 374 $^1/_2$ *frasilas*.

In other respects, too, he did not, in his activity as Sultan, forget his business as a merchant. He sent out his uncle Bushir bin Habib to trade in Ukusu, a district lying to the west. As usual, this commercial journey degenerated into a plundering expedition, and Bushir, together with ten Zanzibaris and fifty Wanyamwezi, paid for the attempt with their lives. They were one and all devoured by the cannibal natives. This again was the signal for a great campaign, conducted by Tippu Tip himself. Even old Kassongo would not be held back from taking part in the expedition. In spite of all representations to the contrary, he insisted on not parting from his long-lost great-nephew; after having lost his two sisters he would not survive their grandson. If Tippu Tip was doomed to die now, he would at least share his fate.

The advance was made with a large force. Tippu Tip declares they had in a few days got together 100,000 men. The number is, of course, exaggerated, for the Arab has no conception of exact computation, besides which he is fond of big-sounding figures. But an imposing levy was no doubt mustered. Killing and burning, as usual, they marched from place to place, and the cruelties elsewhere practised were enhanced by all the male prisoners being devoured, at which the victors developed a hearty appetite, two of them eating up a whole man. Tippu Tip endeavoured to put a stop to these doings-less out of love for his neighbour than because the sickening smell of the slaughtered human flesh upset him. The Manjema, however, paid little heed to his representations. 'If,' they replied, 'we are not to eat men's flesh, do you refrain from goat's flesh.' In face of this reasonable argument things remained as they were. After two months the claims of justice were satisfied, the natives who were left alive paid an indemnity of sixty tusks as a mark of submission, and the victorious army withdrew.

Tippu Tip's absence from Utetera had been utilized by Mkahuja to avenge himself for the defeat inflicted on him. He had raided a village on the frontier, plundering in the usual manner. Thus our hero on returning from one campaign had at once to undertake another. Old Kassongo again accompanied him. This time it was more serious, for the enemy was strong, yet he was overcome within forty days. A large territory was subjugated and much booty in ivory and goats secured.

The supply of ivory now came in very copiously, for the conquered districts had to surrender all the tusks they had. Pange showed himself a very trusty subject, who paid his tribute regularly.

So Tippu Tip spent several years occupied with the duties of a ruler in his own territory and with expeditions, partly peaceful, partly warlike, into the country round. In Marera, a district to the east, two chiefs, Lusuna and Mpiana Nguruwe, vied with each other for his favour. The first, after having made various presents of ivory, sent his brother

Rumwangwa as a regular envoy. He was received by the newly installed Sultan with all honour. In the course of the interview they came to talk of the fact that Tippu Tip's guns were greatly damaged and urgently needed repairs. Then Rumwangwa mentioned that quite close at hand there were countrymen of Tippu Tip's, who would certainly be able to repair the damages. Thus our hero learned by accident that only a few days' march from his place of sojourn there was a flourishing Arab settlement, at Nyangwe, on the Congo.

Naturally he at once became anxious to put himself in communication with his fellow-tribesmen who were so unexpectedly his neighbours, and he set off for Lusuna's country.

On the way, however, his people broke the peace by committing various acts of plunder. Lusuna, out of regard for his powerful ally, winked at the matter, but managed to induce him for the present to remain behind with the bulk of his people; he himself would take a small body with the damaged guns to Nyangwe, and so establish communications.

On the way they were attacked and fired upon by Arabs from Nyangwe, who were just making a raid into the country round. But when they saw that they had not to do with enemies, they parleyed with them and learned that an Arab named Tippu Tip wanted to put himself in communication with them. They had often heard the name, but did not know which of their countrymen was the celebrated bearer of that designation. At their request our hero was fetched, and was at once recognised by them as the famous son of old Mohammed from Tabora.

Arabs with ammunition

Notable Arabs with Colonial Officer

CHAPTER VIII

THE ARAB TOWNS OF NYANGWE AND KASSONGO

'No! here is not any need:
Black the maidens, white the bread !'
GOETHE: *Soldier's Comfort.*

Great was the joy of meeting again, especially for Tippu Tip, who for almost ten years had been cut off from intercourse with his brothers and had no idea how matters stood at home. He learned that Sultan Majid had died meanwhile (1870), and that his brother Bargash, Tippu Tip's enemy, reigned in his stead. He also heard of the great cyclone which in 1872 devastated the island of Zanzibar, tore down houses and uprooted the strongest trees. So, too, it was interesting news to him that political conditions had changed considerably in Tabora. Also they related that a European named Cameron, with whom we shall have to concern ourselves more closely directly, had arrived among them.

The leaders of the Arab host were two men of the coast, Mwinyi Dugumbi and Mtagamoyo. They wanted to take Tippu Tip with them at once to Nyangwe, but he preferred first to settle certain business in his own country, and for the present only sent some men with them to supply verbal proof to the Arab settlement that Hamed bin Mohammed was identical with the celebrated Tippu Tip.

After a few days he followed in person. Nyangwe made on him-accustomed as he had been for years only to native villages-the impression of a prominent capital. And, in fact, it was the *entrepot* for the whole country to a great distance round. It lay, as Cameron recounts, on a hill that secured it from fever, and consisted of two different settlements situated on the right bank of the Congo. The more easterly, which was kept clean, was inhabited by Arabs and the better class of Swahilis; the western-most was the abode of the ordinary people of the coast and the Shensis. Their chief was the Mwinyi Dugumbi mentioned before, whom Cameron describes as a rascal, ruined by drink and sexual excesses.

The Arabs here formed an imposing community. Unlike other countries which they only passed through to plunder, they had established here a secure fastness, in which they might feel themselves at home, and safe from any danger of attack. Here, too, the Arabs' peculiar love for agriculture had again come to the fore. In the well-watered lowlands of the river they had laid out broad rice-fields, which flourished so luxuriantly that people called the whole country New Bengal. Tippu Tip and his people, who for many years had seen no rice, felt their mouths water when they could once more enjoy the old familiar dish.

Soon after our hero's arrival at Nyangwe, the traveller Cameron, who was the first man to cross the Dark Continent, appeared on the scene. Originally an English naval officer, he had been chosen in 1872 by the London Geographical Society to go to the assistance of Livingstone. On March 24, 1873, he started, with three European companions, from Bagamoyo. At Unyanyembe he encountered the body of the great explorer, which was being borne to the coast by his faithful servants. One of Cameron's companions undertook the guidance of the convoy; the two others soon succumbed to the effects of the climate. Cameron marched on alone to Ujiji, which he reached on February 24, 1874. Between March 13 and May 9 he passed round Lake Tanganyika, and discovered in doing so the Lukuga, its westerly outlet to the Lualaba. Proceeding further west on May 18, he arrived in August at Nyangwe, where for a fortnight he endeavoured in vain to procure boats to go down the Lualaba. Although he did not as yet suspect that that stream was the Congo itself, he was convinced from the measurements he had taken that it must be one of its principal tributaries, and could not, as was generally believed, belong to the river system of the Nile.

On August 19 Tippu Tip visited him, and at once, with the chivalry he always showed to European travellers, offered his services for his further journey westwards. He proposed to him to follow him to his camp on the Lomami; from there on he would furnish him with guides, who would be easy to find, as natives in small bodies were constantly in communication with the Sankurru. As it happened, some people from those districts were present and could confirm Tippu Tip's statements.

It must be admitted that the latter's partiality for the European was regarded with great disfavour by his compatriots; but he not only paid no heed to their representations, but allowed himself to be induced by Cameron, who wanted to lose no more time, to make a particularly hasty start. His intention had really been to make a trip shortly to the equally important Arab settlement of Kwa Kassongo,* which lay lower down the river, but he allowed himself to be turned from his purpose by the urgent entreaties of his protege.

On August 26 they set off together, crossed the Ruvubu, passed through various villages laid waste by Arab bands; and though Cameron, owing to violent attacks of fever, could not make the usual marches, they arrived by the 29th at a village of Lusuna's, near which they pitched their camp. Before this they had had a bloody encounter with natives, who recognised in some of the people who had joined the caravan from Nyangwe their old enemies. The intervention of Tippu Tip, however, who was everywhere feared, soon restored peace.

They rested for some days near the village where Lusuna was staying just then, as Tippu Tip had various matters to discuss with his ally. Lusuna came backwards and forwards on visits to the camp; still more often did his wives, whose remarkable beauty had made a particular impression on the English traveller. They gradually became very confiding, and a busy intercourse sprang up between the township and the stranger's camp.

---

*The place was really called Mwana Mamba, but, because a Kassongo ruled there, was mostly styled by the Arabs Kwa (Big) Kassongo, and later simply Kassongo.

Lusuna was in the habit of bringing with him on his visits a special carved chair, and using the lap of one of his wives as a footstool.

On their onward march the caravan came to a township, which was the chief's real capital and inhabited by him and his wives. Lusuna's marriage relations were, according to Tippu Tip's account, a remarkable freak of polygamy. Of actual wives he had thirty, who lived with him in his homestead. The other women inhabitants of the place also counted as his wives, only they were legally entitled to provide themselves with other domestic companions. The children born of them were reckoned in any case as Lusuna's offspring, and might attain to the throne like his actual offspring. On September 3 Tippu Tip's camp was reached. It was situated very favourably on a low eminence. In spite of its temporary character, it had pleasant houses, of which one with two living-rooms and a bathroom was set apart for the European guest.

Soon after their arrival Kassongo announced his visit, which was awaited in an open hall built for gatherings. The Arabs put on their garments of state in honour of the chief. Cameron as a tattered traveller could not appear in gala costume. He dwells on this with regret, and is quite right in his instinct if he sees a shortcoming in his shabby clothing. Man in a state of nature makes a great deal of an imposing exterior, and among the indispensable paraphernalia of an explorer should certainly be numbered a few garments of ceremony. Zintgraff, the explorer of the Cameroons, after he had realized this necessity, had a white silk burnous made for state occasions; while Peters, in his Emin Pasha expedition, devised a fancy uniform bedizened with gold in order to impress the Masai.

Cameron's account of his visit is as follows:* 'An individual authorized by the chief to do duty as master of the ceremonies then arrived, carrying a long carved walking-stick as a badge of office, his appearance being the signal for all porters and slaves in camp and people from surrounding villages to crowd round to witness the spectacle. The master of the ceremonies drove the anxious sightseers back, and formed a space near the reception-room-as the hut may be termed-and their different subchiefs arrived, each followed by spearmen and shield-bearers, varying in number according to rank, a few of the most important being followed also by drummers.

'Each new-comer was brought to the entrance, where the Arabs and myself had taken our seats, and his name and rank proclaimed by the master of the ceremonies, who further informed him the position he was to occupy in order to be ready to welcome Kassongo. After some time spent in this manner, much drumming and shouting announced the approach of the great man himself. First in the procession were half a dozen drummers; then thirty or forty spearmen, followed by six women carrying shields; and next Kassongo, accompanied by his brothers, eldest son, two of his daughters, and a few officials about him, the rear being brought up by spearmen, drummers, and *marimba*-players.

'On his reaching the entrance to the hut, a ring was formed, and Kassongo-dressed in a jacket and kilt of red and yellow woollen fabric, trimmed with longhaired monkey-skins (a present from Tippu Tip), and with a greasy handkerchief tied round his

---

*'Across Africa,' 1877, vol. ii., p. 21.

head-performed a jigging dance with his two daughters.

'The terpsichorean performance being concluded in about a quarter of an hour, he then entered the hut, and we had a long conversation.'

Cameron informed the chief that he wanted to cross the Lomami and proceed to the Sankurru, which he believed to be a lake, and Kassongo readily offered to help him by negotiations with the Sultan of the territory to be traversed. However, the answer sent back by him was that 'no strangers with guns had ever passed through his country, and that none should do so without fighting their way.'

The European was not disposed to risk forcing his way through, though with Tippu Tip's help he felt himself strong enough to do so, but luckily it proved possible to reach his goal by a circuitous route. He learned from various quarters that Portuguese traders had arrived at the capital of Urua, to the south-west of his present place of sojourn. As a proof of the truth of this statement, an old Portuguese soldier's coat was shown him, which a native had recently received from one of the white men.

So Cameron decided as his next step to get into touch with these Portuguese, and Tippu Tip gave him three guides, who journeyed ten days with him on the road. He reached the capital of Urua, and found there Portuguese half-castes, who, although Christians, were carrying on a brisk trade in slaves. Indeed, they behaved much more cruelly than their Arab fellow-traders, to whom no religious injunction of love for one's neighbour forbids this traffic as sin. After eventful journeys in the southern districts-which Tippu Tip had passed through before-Cameron arrived with his Portuguese companions, more dead than alive, at Benguela, on the West Coast, in November, 1875, and thus completed the first crossing of Africa-a meritorious exploit, rich in geographical results.

After his men returned, Tippu Tip had waited three months longer in his camp, so as to be able to help Cameron in case he came back unsuccessful. As, however, nothing further was heard of him, he departed to attend once more to his duties as ruler and to his business affairs.

To begin with, he wanted to make the journeys, already planned, but given up on Cameron's account, to Kwa Kassongo, where dwelt many of his friends from Zanzibar. Above all he looked forward to meeting again his cousin, Mohammed bin Said-who died lately at an advanced age in Zanzibar-known far and wide as Bwana Nzige (Master Locust), a name given him because his caravans were as large as swarms of locusts, and ate bare all the districts that they passed through.

As Kassongo Rushie had abdicated once and for all, and was glad to have nothing more to do with the business of government, our hero before leaving Utetera had to appoint a representative there. He chose for the post a man of the coast named Mwinyi Dadi, with whom he left a body of a hundred Wanyamwezi with fifty guns.

Guided by some of Kassongo's men, Tippu Tip first made his way to Nyangwe. The Arabs there wanted at all costs to induce him to remain with them, so as to have the support of his powerful armed force in their constant collisions with the African tribes around; but he would not be persuaded, even when they warned him that there was famine at Kwa Kassongo. As a born fatalist, he believed that if he went there Allah, the Lord of Might, would order all for the best.

THE ARAB TOWNS OF NYANGWE AND KASSONGO

At Kwa Kassongo the chief command over all the Arabs was at once conferred on him. He found that the people of Nyangwe had only told the truth about the unfavourable state of things in the place. Provisions were scarce, and the natives around showed themselves hostile. The latter fact he had occasion shortly to experience personally, as 200 of his slaves were suddenly carried off.

This gave the welcome pretext for a great campaign. True, the Arabs were not well provided with weapons, but under the leadership of the ever victorious Tippu Tip they feared nothing. The Shensis were speedily vanquished, and had once more to pay heavy tribute; in particular, they were forced to deliver up all their ivory. After peace was restored agriculture once more flourished. There was so much rice that the people of Nyangwe came over to buy it, and paid a heavy price for it in ivory. Tribes that lay further away were also subjugated, so that all the way to Utetera things were so peaceful that even women could pass to and fro without risk.

Utetera itself proved to be a regular gold-mine. Mwinyi Dadi saw to the affairs of his master so excellently that he could regularly send ample supplies of ivory.

From Kwa Kassongo Tippu Tip for the first time reopened communications with his old father and other friends at Tabora. Their joy was great when they heard of the prosperity of the long-absent one. His messengers found Mohammed bin Masoud, his stepbrother, also at Tabora. Tippu Tip, as we know, left him behind at Itahua with Nsama. After hearing nothing for years of the brother who had journeyed so far away, he had returned to the Arab town. During that time he had acquired 700 *frasilas* of ivory, and passed them on in Tippu Tip's name to his creditor, Taria Topan.

His compatriots at Tabora sent the messengers back with various gifts, and requested Tippu Tip to come home as soon as possible. But as trade was just going well he could not make up his mind to return, in spite of repeated persuasions. Most of the Tabora messengers settled down in the new country, became petty Sultans, and were so pleased with their position that they never thought of going home again.

When all messages had thus proved fruitless, Said bin Ali at last came himself to bring his friend away. As will be remembered, this Arab had parted from Tippu Tip in Urua, in order to trade in Katanga with Sultan Msire. When his merchandise had come to an end, he had got into communication with Mohammed bin Masoud, and proceeded in company with him to Tabora.

When he now arrived at Kassongo, Tippu Tip had just gone down the Congo on a trading trip. At the news of Said's coming he at once turned back, and at length allowed himself to be persuaded to go to Tabora together with his friend. But before he could carry out this intention fresh warlike occurrences demanded his attention. The Portuguese traders whom Cameron met in the south of Urua had invaded Utetera, and robbed and plundered there. Tippu Tip marched against them and defeated them.

On his return to Nyangwe he received the sad news that his true friend, Said bin Ali, the companion of so many years of wandering, rich alike in privations and successes, had died. During the course of the expedition news had been brought that he had fallen dangerously ill of blood-poisoning.

So the return to Tabora again receded into the distant future.

Colonial Officer in a village

Porters carrying Ivory

CHAPTER IX

WITH STANLEY DOWN THE CONGO

'La abrah hatta ablur magma el baharen au amdhi hukuban.'
'I shall not cease until I reach the junction of the two seas, even if I have to journey for eighty years.'-
KORAN: Suret el Kahaf, xviii. 62.

Some months went by in peaceful work at Nyangwe and Kwa Kassongo, when one day the traveller Stanley appeared on his famous journey across Africa. His arrival turned the activity of our hero for the next few months into fresh channels.

Stanley was born, in 1841, in Wales, of humble parentage. His real name was James Rowland, but he was afterwards adopted at New Orleans, where he went as a cabin-boy, by an American merchant and took his name. He travelled as a newspaper correspondent through Turkey, Asia Minor, and Abyssinia. In 1869 Bennett, the proprietor of the *New York Herald*, sent him to Africa to look for the long lost Livingstone. He found him at Ujiji on November 10, 1871. In company with him, he travelled round Lake Tanganyika, and then returned home by Zanzibar, while Livingstone remained at Unyanyembe. This journey had established his reputation as an African explorer. After having taken part in the Ashanti Campaign in 1873-1874, he was secured by the managers of the *New York Herald* and *Daily Telegraph*, who shared the expenses, for a new journey in Africa. Starting from Bagamoyo, he marched, in November, 1874, to the Victoria Nyanza, which he reached in February, 1875. In January, 1876, he visited Mtesa, King of Uganda. That prince placed 2,000 spearmen at his disposal for his further march to Lake Albert. The goal which Stanley reached under this escort was, however, though he was not aware of it, the hitherto undiscovered Lake Albert Edward. From there the explorer turned aside by way of the territory of Karagwe to Lake Tanganyika, which he circumnavigated for the second time, in June and July, 1876. At the end of August he started from Ujiji for the west, and in October reached Kassongo, where, among numerous other Arabs, he found our hero.

The autobiographer describes this first meeting in the following very dramatic fashion:

'At the end of another month Stanley appeared one afternoon. I bade him welcome, and we allotted him a house. Next morning we visited him and he showed us a gun and said: "With this gun you can fire fifteen shots at a time." But we knew nothing of a fifteen-shot gun; we had neither heard of such a thing nor seen one. I asked him: "From one barrel?" And he replied: "They come out of one barrel." Then I said to him: "Fire it off, that we may see." But he said: "I will sooner pay twenty or thirty dollars than fire off a single cartridge." Then I thought in my heart: "He is lying. That is a rifle with one barrel, and the second thing there must be the ramrod.* How can the bullets come one after another out of the one barrel?" And I told him in turn: "On the Lomami is a bow on which you place twenty arrows, and when you shoot it off all twenty fly at once, and every arrow strikes a man."† Then he rose at once, went outside and fired twelve shots. He also seized a pistol and let off six shots. After this he came back and seated himself on the *barasa*. We were mightily astonished. I begged him, "Show me how you load." Then he showed me.'

Stanley makes no mention of this firing story, which made such a remarkable impression on Tippu Tip, who, like all Arabs, is a great lover of weapons. But the life-like picture he gives of our hero is well worth reading.‡

'He was a tall, black-bearded man of negroid complexion, in the prime of life, straight and quick in his movements, a picture of energy and strength. He had a fine, intelligent face, with a nervous twitching of the eyes, and gleaming white, perfectly formed teeth. He was attended by a large retinue of young Arabs, who looked up to him as chief, and a score of Wangwana and Wanyamwezi followers, whom he had led over thousands of miles through Africa.

'With the air of a well-bred Arab and almost courtier-like in his manner, he welcomed me to Mwana Wambe's village, and, his slaves being ready at hand with mat and bolster, he reclined *vis-á-vis*, while a buzz of admiration of his style was perceptible from the onlookers.

'After regarding him for a few minutes I came to the conclusion that this Arab was a remarkable man, the most remarkable that I had met among Arabs, Wa-Swahili, and half-castes in Africa. He was neat in his person: his clothes were of a spotless white, his fez-cap brand-new, his waist was encircled by a rich *dowle* (dagger-belt), his dagger was splendid with silver filigree, and his *tout ensemble* was that of an Arab gentleman in very comfortable circumstances.'

Stanley's first questions were about the fate of Cameron, who, aiming at the same goal as himself, had at this point abandoned the direction he had kept hitherto and turned off southwards. What particularly interested him was to learn for what reasons his predecessor had left the course of the river.

Tippu Tip explained this to him clearly and intelligibly. It was the difficulty in procuring boats, the threat of hostilities on the part of the natives of the districts they would have to pass through, and the disinclination of his own followers to risk their lives on a river whose channel was difficult to navigate and whose course was quite unknown.

With these obstacles, which many years before had forced Livingstone to turn back, Stanley would also have to contend. Like Cameron before him, he endeavoured to secure

---

*What the narrator takes for the second barrel is the magazine.

†This answer is quite in keeping with Tippu Tip's ironical way. As he thinks Stanley is romancing, he wants to outdo him by a still bigger lie.

‡'Through the Dark Continent,' vol. ii., pp. 95, 96.

the powerful assistance of the King of Mamyema, but at first he showed little inclination and excused himself by the fact that at the time he had scarcely 300 warriors with him. These would indeed be enough to go with Stanley, who had a strong force of his own; but when by-and-by he would have to return without him, he would surely be annihilated. The Shensis, when they saw, as they would, his troops coming back alone and with empty hands, would say that the powerful Tippu Tip's caravan had been scattered by hostile tribes, and would do their utmost to complete its destruction.

To Stanley's objection that he himself was going to face a still more hazardous future, the Arab coolly rejoined that it was his own personal pleasure if it amused him to risk his life for the discovery of mountains, lakes, and rivers; he himself was a plain ivory-trader, and had no fancy for such unprofitable tricks. At last, however, he went so far as to say that he would sleep over the matter once more.

The next morning, towards eight o'clock, the discussion was continued, and Stanley was requested to set forth his plans in more detail. He replied that he intended to go down-stream in boats until the river took a marked turn either northwards or westwards.

'How far was this by the land route?'

He did not know; perhaps Tippu Tip did.

'No,' replied the latter, 'but I have brought a man with me who has been further down-stream than anyone else.'

The man in question, Abed bin Juma by name, then informed the astonished Stanley that the river flowed northwards and yet further northwards, until at last it emptied itself into the sea. To be sure, he could not say what sea it was; it could, however, if he was right about it, only be the Mediterranean.

Asked for the source of his knowledge, he told a wonderful story which, although swarming with geographical impossibilities, yet doubtless had a nucleus of truth. It was that on a predatory expedition headed by Mtagamoyo, the fearless leader of the Nyangwe men, after days of marching they had come to the country of the Wakuma, to the west of Lomami. There they had found some representatives of that mysterious race of dwarfs whose existence had long been regarded as a fable, until at length, in 1876, du Chaillu, first among Europeans, found similar pigmies on the Gaboon. The first scientific investigations touching them we owe to Stuhlmann, who in 1893 brought with him to Europe two Batua women from the district west of Ruwenzori. They are scattered from the sources of the Ituri throughout the basin of the Congo as far as the lower course of the Sankurru. They live in groups among the other tribes, with whom they have little intercourse. They inhabit thick forests and live by hunting, which they carry on with poisoned arrows. Their stature never exceeds 4 feet 10 inches, and it is supposed that together with the Bushmen, with whom they have many points of resemblance, they represent the aboriginal race of Africa.

The dwarfs whom the Arabs met said that in their country there were boundless treasures of ivory. They themselves attached no value to it, and even wondered why foreigners wanted it, as it was not good to eat. Enticed further by these fabulous narratives, Mtagamoyo's caravan after six more days' march reached the land of the dwarfs proper, but was very fiercely received by the malicious little demons. They sprang from the soil around like mushrooms, and showered their poisoned arrows on the travellers, causing them endless losses. Only thirty were able to escape with their lives. In addition to this, Abed told harrowing stories of apes as big as men and frightful snakes.

The route by the river was not less dangerous. Below Nyangwe it was a mass of cataracts, which would bring certain destruction to any vessel. Old Daud (Livingstone) had turned back precisely on this account, and no one would induce the Arab to return to those terrible regions.

In spite of this weird description, Stanley, whose account we are following for the present, persisted in his plan, and Tippu Tip showed himself not averse to it. He first told all the Arabs, with the exception of his cousin Mohammed bin Said, to go outside, and then stated his conditions. His countrymen had indeed urgently dissuaded him from risking his life, but he did not want to place Stanley in a dilemma, and so was ready, for a consideration of 5,000 dollars, to accompany him sixty days' march, reckoning four hours to each day.

The following points were agreed upon:

1. The starting-point of the journey to be Nyangwe; the day and the direction taken to be determined by Stanley.

2. The journey not to last longer than three months.

3. The rate of travel to be two days' marching to one day of rest.

4. After Tippu Tip had accompanied him sixty marches of four hours each, Stanley was to return with him to Nyangwe, unless he met traders from the West Coast on the way, whom he might join and continue his march to the Atlantic. In that case Stanley was to engage himself to hand over two thirds of his own men to Tippu Tip as an escort on the return march to Nyangwe.

5. Exclusive of the 5,000 dollars, Stanley was to pay for the keep of 140 of Tippu Tip's men during their absence from Kassongo, going and returning.

6. If, owing to the difficulties of the country or the attitude of the natives, he should find it impracticable to continue the journey, he would still have to pay the full sum of 5,000 dollars.

7. In case Tippu Tip should abandon Stanley through faint-heartedness before the expiration of the stipulated time, he was to forfeit all claim to reward or payment for keep.

So far Stanley, from whose statements Tippu Tip's accounts differ materially. He says that Stanley came to him as a suppliant, and begged and entreated him to accompany him to 'Munza,' a country situated eighty days' march from there in the direction of Mecca-*i.e.*, north-north-east-and he would give him 7,000 dollars (not 5,000); and that no mention was made at that time of the plan of travelling by the river. Tippu Tip replied that he was not indisposed to come with him, but that he was not doing it out of greed of gold, for he possessed so much ivory that 7,000 dollars were not a consideration to him; if he went it would principally be out of desire to oblige.

He says that the next morning he declared his readiness to go, but that he did not agree to the conditions recapitulated by Stanley in the manner set forth above; least of all did any written compact pass between them.

He also emphasizes the fact that his fellow-tribesmen strongly advised him against going, and when they saw he had made up his mind, reproached him violently. He must have gone quite mad, they said, to endanger his life to please an unbeliever. Did he want to become a European himself? But he answered them with dignity: 'Perhaps I am mad and it is you who are sane. Mind your own concerns.'

It is plain that the accounts are widely divergent. With regard to the sum agreed on-whether 5,000 or 7,000 dollars-perhaps Stanley is the more worthy of credence. The Arab has, as has before been insisted on, little comprehension for figures and loves to exaggerate, while Stanley had no reason to put the amount really promised too low, for he never paid it, as we shall see later on.

However, it is one man's word against another's, and as the negotiation was carried on without the presence of witnesses, it is difficult to decide which of the two accounts is the correct one.

The greater advantage in the alleged compact lay in any case with Stanley. His enterprise would perhaps have been wrecked by the ill-will of the Arab, while the latter would have managed without the 5,000 or 7,000 dollars, and did so manage in the long-run.

Stanley then tells us a pathetic story, embellished with a dramatic night scene, in which he debated with his servant Frank whether they should choose the route which seemed more dangerous, but was more in harmony with the object of their journey along the line of the river, or that which Cameron had adopted through Kassongo's country; and how they at last decided to settle it by the spin of a coin. A rupee was produced and spun-'head' for the river, 'tail' for the land. 'Tail' came down twice. The straws also, which were next called on for their oracle, gave their voice for the land route. In spite of which the daring travellers decided to follow the course of the river.

After these jests, the description of which displays Stanley's bravado in the proper light, the morning of October 23, 1874, dawned, on which day, according to the English version, the contract was signed and the details agreed to-viz., that Tippu Tip should take with him on the journey 140 armed and 70 reserve men.

On the 24th they marched from Kassongo to Nyangwe, where Tippu Tip assembled his men and got them ready for the route. He had in the end, including women and children, a train of 700 souls. Of these, however, 400 belonged to Stanley's following; the remainder were only to proceed for a few days in company with the main body, after which they were to diverge in a north-easterly direction, in order to trade in districts as yet unvisited.

On November 5 the caravan left Nyangwe, and in the afternoon, after journeying a distance of nine and a half miles over a rolling plain covered with grass, reached the villages of Na-Kasimbi, in which they made their first halt. On the 6th they found themselves in face of Mitamba, a thick, black forest, in whose shade, which no ray of sunlight illumined, the travellers were swallowed up. He who has not seen with his own eyes a tropical primeval forest can scarcely form an idea of the horrors of such a wilderness. There is none of the refreshing breath of our native forests; a stifling, mouldy atmosphere meets the intruder. Between stout and gigantic trees wind creepers as high as a man, which mock the axe as laboriously it seeks to make its way, and grasp with their octopus-like arms at the garments of the wanderer, who worms his way through the less matted spots. The primeval tree-trunks, disturbed in their sleep, shake down their dew in great drops, and the groping foot seeks vainly for a firm hold on the viscous soil.

Stanley was spared none of these difficulties, and his course was still further hampered by the numerous streams, carrying more or less water, that had to be passed. In spite of this, nine to ten miles a day were covered, though the carriers often did not reach the camping-ground till late in the evening. Those among them who had to carry the parts of a steel boat that Stanley took with him fared particularly badly. The sections could not always be reduced to the dimensions of an average load-which should not exceed 60 pounds-but had in some instances to be made into double loads, and in the closely-tangled undergrowth, through which a single man could scarcely worm his way, it was a heavy task to make progress with them. The stipulation that they were only to march four hours a day soon fell into disuse over it.

On November 11 the boat-carriers did not reach camp at all; they only came in at noon the next day, completely exhausted.

Of course, under all these adverse conditions, the mood of the caravan was from the first most depressed, and degenerated from day to day into open discontent, the more so as the few who had followed this route before declared that the terrors with which they had so far made acquaintance were child's play to what was yet to come. The most rebellious were naturally the men with the boat, whose complaints, justified as Stanley could not but own they were, found a loud echo among the others. Even Tippu Tip sighs at the recollection of the labours of those marches, and among his followers there was open murmuring, which reached Stanley's ears, against the 'Forest of the Infidel,' as, with a certain double meaning directed against the leader, they christened the jungle they were passing through.

On November 14 the 300 men of the trading caravan took leave of them and marched away in a north-easterly direction. After a further very trying march-so Stanley relates-on the morning of the 16th the remainder announced through Tippu Tip their determination to turn back. The forest through which they were now passing was not made for travel; only vile pagans, monkeys, and wild beasts could harbour in it.

After two hours' debate, in which Stanley exerted all his eloquence, he succeeded apparently in inducing Tippu Tip to accompany him further. It was decided to strike off to the river, and march along its left bank. Tippu Tip pledged himself, setting aside the first contract, to twenty more marches from their present camping-ground, in return for a wage of 2,600 dollars, and it was decided to discuss later a possible further extension.

Tippu Tip's statements here again vary widely from Stanley's version. He says that the American, in face of the difficulties of the march and the unwillingness of the carriers, lost his head completely, and himself made the proposal to diverge to the Congo. He entirely disputes any reversal of the compact, to which he had from the first given only a qualified assent, let alone the lowering of the wage promised him. However that may be, on November 19 the river was reached, forty-one geographical miles north of Nyangwe. It was about 1,200 yards wide, and no longer bore the name Lualaba, as at Nyangwe. Stanley, not yet knowing that he had to do with the Congo, called it from this point on the Livingstone.

After the camp had been pitched they began to put together the steel boat known as the *Lady Alice*. Meanwhile Stanley stretched himself in the grass on the river-bank, and as, full of grave thoughts, he contemplated the waters flowing past him into an unknown distance, the resolution ripened in him at all hazards to navigate their hitherto uncharted course in boats, regardless where they might flow.

At once he summoned his people together in order to deliver to them a stirring address. To show the reader how skilful he was in handling the natives, true to his old journalistic calling, he gives this speech, which is worthy of embodiment in an epic, in two pages of print, with all theatrical accessories. Of course, the effect of his words is that at once half the at first hesitating blacks swear to follow him blindly to the death; only Tippu Tip and a couple of other Arabs stand aside as an obstinately dissentient element, and endeavour to dissuade him from his daring project.

He is already in a fair way to convince these also by the all-mastering power of his eloquence, when the palaver is interrupted by the appearance of several canoes full of natives. Stanley tried, by the help of an interpreter, to persuade them of his peaceful intentions; but when they heard that the new-comers were from Nyangwe, their mistrust was doubly excited. Even the promise of presents of untold beads could not induce them to bring their boats in and take the travellers to the further bank. On the contrary, they at once raised their war-cry, which found a hundred echoes in the bushes on the river-banks.

Meanwhile the steel boat had been put together, and Stanley crossed to the left bank to open relations in person. The Shensis at length declared themselves willing to enter into friendly intercourse with the new-comers, on condition that the white man should contract blood-brotherhood with their chieftain. An island in the middle of the river was fixed on as the scene of the solemnity, the time to be next morning.

Such proposals of fraternization on the part of natives for the most part amount to a clumsy snare. This Stanley suspected, so as a precaution he landed a considerable body of men on the island during the night. His servant Frank was sent as white man for the completion of the ceremony, while he himself remained hard by with the boat, to be ready at once in case of treachery.

He was not deceived in his forebodings. From the first the Shensis adopted a threatening attitude, and soon proceeded to open hostilities. But when they were confronted by the reserves that had been concealed during the night, they hastily took to flight and paddled back to the left bank.

After the failure of this attempt at peaceful relations, Stanley decided at all hazards to transfer his caravan to the west bank. As many men as the *Lady Alice* would carry, thirty in round numbers, were taken across to begin with; while they set to work to entrench a camp, the remaining carriers were gradually fetched, and at length several Shensis were induced by a bribe of beads to place six boats at their disposal for transport purposes. By night on November 20 Stanley's whole caravan was encamped on the left bank.

By the next morning the hard-won friendship of the natives was again at an end; all the villages far and wide were deserted, and so it remained for the most part during the ensuing march.

Stanley, with a few men, proceeded down-stream in the *Lady Alice*; the main body followed by the land route. Both parties had unpleasant experiences in the shape of hostilities on the part of the dwellers on the banks, but the land detachment came off worse, as it lost its way and had to sustain an engagement with the Bakusu, with much loss. Not till November 26 did the two parties effect a junction, after which they kept more in touch.

In course of time they succeeded in getting together a certain number of native boats, which were very serviceable, as small-pox and dysentery broke out in the land division, and made many men unfit for marching. A floating hospital was formed for them.

The two accounts again differ greatly as to the way in which the boats were procured. Tippu Tip, who is generally inclined to excuse his sins on the ground of necessity, declares with praiseworthy candour that the canoes were captured in a boisterous 'drive.' He writes:

'I attacked the Shensis, and took their boats and goats from them. Every day I got six or seven canoes, and any number of goats. But the inhabitants are very well trained in making off with their boats. They have also war-drums, called *mingungu*. The first town beats them, then the second follows suit, and every town that hears the signal passes it on. Thus one may travel for two months without finding any people in the townships. You only see goats, for there are very many of them, and they cannot get away. And most of the boats are small, and one does not easily get them unless the occupants hear bullets flying about their ears or are actually hit by them. Then they plunge into the water and leave the boats behind them.'

It is easy for Tippu Tip to be outspoken over this episode, for he knows that the European reader is bound to lay the responsibility on Stanley. The latter, however, in full consciousness of innocence, disdains to invoke the plea of necessity, well-grounded though it was, and describes to us how he obtained lawful possession of the boats in a perfectly peaceable manner. In the first instance six masterless canoes were found and appropriated, while on December 4 they discovered a very large boat that had clearly been abandoned for years; this, though much damaged, was also annexed, and, after the most urgent defects had been repaired, could carry sixty persons.

These pieces of luck of course materially facilitated their advance, but for all that there were difficulties enough, while sickness and the hostility of the natives gave them no respite. More lives were lost daily. On the 11th eight corpses, among them the three youthful favourites of our hero, were sunk in the waters of the fatal stream. In the middle of December the river wing had a serious encounter near the village of Vinya Nyaza, which might easily have been fatal, but was turned into a victory by the timely arrival of the land wing. The Shensis took to flight, and in pursuing them thirty-eight canoes, mostly quite good ones, were taken.

On December 22 formal peace was concluded, and the long-desired blood-brotherhood accomplished. The Shensis received back twenty-five boats; the remainder were retained as a suitable indemnity. Stanley was now sufficiently provided with boats to dispense with further help from Tippu Tip. They agreed to part here, somewhat above the mouth of the Kasuku.

As to the manner of their agreement the accounts again differ fundamentally. Stanley declares that Tippu Tip expressed to him so categorically his intention of turning back at this point that he abandoned all attempts at talking him over, although, according to the last compact, the Arab chief was still bound for eight days' march.

The latter, on the contrary, asserts that Stanley, after thanking him heartily for the support so far accorded him, himself suggested his return, as he had boats enough to proceed alone. All he had stipulated with him was that Tippu Tip should steal two larger boats, in which he could conveniently ship his riding asses; and this *coup* they had carried out together with great success.

On one point the two narrators agree-that the condition was made that Tippu Tip should exert his influence to induce Stanley's men under all circumstances to continue the march. Stanley is silent as to how this influence was brought to bear, while our autobiographer gives the following delightful description:

'Hereupon Stanley summoned his men and said to them: "Hamed bin Mohammed will turn back at this point. But do you make ready. The day after to-morrow we shall start." Then the men answered him: "If Hamed bin Mohammed turns back, we shall all turn back. We are not going into unknown regions. We engaged on the coast for two years, and now it is two years and a half. If Hamed bin Mohammed turns back, we shall certainly turn back too." And all the men persisted obstinately that they would not go further. Then Stanley became very mournful; even his food was no longer tasteful to him, and he was on the point of weeping.

'In the evening he came to me and said: "My whole labour is lost if these men turn back. Then I too must turn back, and my toil has been in vain, Help me now, I implore you." I said to him: "God willing, I will help you under all circumstances!"

'I lay down to sleep, and next morning visited him and asked: "What have you decided?" He replied: "I have decided nothing, and I don't know what I am to do." Then I said to him: "Well now, follow my advice. Assemble all your people, then call me and speak to me with harsh words, and say: "If you go back all my people will turn back. They cannot do otherwise. Now, my work is for the State, and that is no other than Seyyid Bargash. If my people turn back, I must turn back too. Then I shall tell the Sultan that it was Hamed bin Mohammed who made my further journey impossible. Then the State will confiscate your goods. When you have said that it is well, then I shall speak." Then I went away.

'In the afternoon he sent for me and called together his people, and spoke to me in presence of his men in harsh words, as I had prompted him. Thereupon I said to them: "You have heard Stanley's words; now get you on your way and depart. Whoever follows me I will kill; for you would plunge in ruin and my property would be confiscated by Government. Then I should be as good as dead. My toil during many years would be in vain. Should I not certainly perish here? If you follow me, I will kill you." Thereupon I withdrew and they went their way.

'Towards evening came Stanley's people, and their leaders said to me: "Our time with this European is over; we positively must turn back." I said to them: "Your words are idle-march on." Then said they: "Do you wish us to perish?" I answered them: "As it is with him so it will be with you. If you are lost you will be lost together." Then they said:

"This European is a churl. He gives us nothing without putting it down-not even clothes does he give us; not a single loin-fabric does he give." I said to them: "Let that be my care. I will give you as much as you want. Only go on." Then they answered me: "What, then, are we to do? We are now afraid of you, because of the words you have spoken. But with this European we have nothing to do. Our time was up more than six months ago." But I said to them: "Your words are idle. Do as I tell you."'

Then, according to Tippu Tip's autobiography, Stanley at his instance gave his men nine loads of garments, and thus won them, by gentle compulsion, to accompany him further.

Although Stanley leaves these small details unmentioned, he describes all the more minutely the rewards which he bestowed on Tippu Tip and his men. Thus our hero received a voucher for 2,600 dollars, a riding ass, a chest, a gold chain, a revolver, ammunition, and great store of beads, copper wire, and clothes. His followers, according to their rank, received from I to 20 *dotis* of material for clothing.

Tippu Tip in his autobiography says not a word of these presents of Stanley's, though he admitted to the author verbally that he received a draft for money, but the amount was not communicated to him, and as he cannot read English he could not learn what it was. He sent the cheque to his business friend Taria Topan to be cashed, and was highly astonished to receive only 2,000-3,000 dollars on it, instead of the expected 7,000. He disputes having received the presents enumerated by Stanley; only as regards the donkey, he does admit that he received two. Stanley had, it seems, four riding asses, of which he took the two best with him. He could not ship the other two, and so gave them away. The fabrics that Stanley enumerates as presented to him and his men were really so given, but were not gratuitous. They represented the payment of the keep, which, according to compact, Stanley was to supply for the return of the escort. But he had indeed made him lying promises, and said:

'I do not know how I can possibly repay your goodness, nor do I know what I am to give you in money. For when I return to Europe I shall receive high honours and much money. I will present you with a watch worth 1,000 dollars, with diamonds, and how much money I shall give you I cannot reckon.'

Finally Stanley begged him to wait for a month where he was, to be at hand with help in case he should be forced to turn back.

The last two days chanced to be Christmastide, and were devoted to harmless amusements, so as to distract Stanley's band from the feelings incident to parting, and drive away the cares arising from an uncertain future. The captured canoes received the proud titles of English war-ships, and raced against each other, the winning crew receiving prizes. Foot races also were held, and even the stately Tippu Tip did not disdain to take part in the sport. The village street, 300 yards in length, was made into a course, on which the Arab chieftain and Frank the servant tested their swiftness of foot. Tippu Tip was first at the winning-post with a lead of 15 yards, and received a prize of a silver drinking-cup. Races between lads, and even dusky ladies, formed further items in the enlivening programme. A war-dance by the Wanyamwezi, whose deeptoned drums and shrill fifes sent a strange Christmas music into the stillness of the primeval forest, wound up the festal day.

On the second day of holiday-making Tippu Tip gave a banquet to the whole caravan.

The rice and roast mutton were freely washed down with palm wine, in the forbidden fire of which the last cares for the future were drowned.

On December 27, 1876, Stanley with his following began the further march into the unknown, and at the beginning of August, 1877, reached the West Coast. The principal result of his crossing of Africa, rich as it was in other respects, was that it decided beyond dispute the question of the source of the Congo.

Locals with record Ivory Tusks in Zanzibar

CHAPTER X

BY TABORA BACK TO ZANZIBAR

'I had no more than this staff when I passed over this Jordan; and now I am two hosts.'- GEN. xxxii. 10.

Tippu Tip waited for a month, according to his promise, at the place where Stanley had parted with him, and then marched to the lower Lomami, where he found very advantageous trading conditions.

The natives of those parts had, indeed, no conception that ivory was an object of value. They hunted elephants, it is true, but only for the sake of their flesh; the tusks were for the most part heedlessly thrown away into the bush, where they rotted or were devoured by insects. Here and there the Shensis took them, and turned them to strange uses in the villages. Artists who had a glimmering of the high value of this important product fashioned flutes and household utensils out of it; ivory mortars were common, in which bananas, a leading article of food of these tribes, were mashed up. It was also a favourite plan to plant the tusks in the ground as a fence round the homestead. One can fancy how the Arabs' hearts beat high when they passed such a precious fencing.

As an equivalent for the ivory, copper was given, which Tippu Tip had acquired by barter at Utetera. He had bought 5 *frasilas* of that metal there for a *frasila* of beads. Half a *frasila* he had presented to Stanley at parting; for the remainder he now obtained 200 *frasilas* of ivory. A *frasila* of beads cost at the time he purchased it in Zanzibar 3 dollars, while he could sell that weight of ivory for at least 50 dollars. So his 3 dollars had turned into 10,000.

The departure entailed many fresh combats, and the caravan had often to suffer from the poisoned arrows of the Shensis, although there were not so many fatal wounds as before, for the men had learned from Stanley that the wounds must be at once cauterized to avoid the effect of the poison.

Only when the camp was pitched in the immediate neighbourhood of the river had they any peace, for the dwellers on the banks had a lively recollection of the former encounters, and fled hastily to the islands when the travellers came near.

At Kassongo Tippu Tip found the situation most favourable, and, what was most important for him, the tributes of ivory from the conquered districts had flowed in abundantly. By his subjects he was received with jubilation; they had been distressed at his lengthy absence, and now the news spread like wild-fire through his whole domain that he had come back safe and sound.

As to the two next years, he has not much to record: they went by monotonously with expeditions-some peaceful, some warlike-in the country. He appointed his cousin Mohammed bin Said, who had grown tired of the nomad life, regent in Utetera, where he was so much at ease that he could not wish for anything better; 'for the Shensis of those regions are good-hearted, the women are fair, and the country is fruitful.'

In the middle of 1879 our hero was again reminded of his home by messengers from Zanzibar. Sultan Bargash sent him by letter a summons to return at once, as his banker, Taria Topan, wished to settle accounts with him. The two years for which the advances were made had by now grown to twelve, and his business friend must be kept waiting no longer.

In order to give this missive, which was couched in very friendly terms, quite an official character, the Sultan sent with it a valuable present-a modern repeating rifle. The gift was all the more flattering as Tippu Tip had not as yet had the honour of making the giver's acquaintance. Taria, who also gave him a rifle, wrote in the same strain as the Sultan, and added the news that Stanley had some time before (November 26, 1877) returned to Zanzibar, and had said a great deal about his friend Tippu Tip. There was a letter from him, too, and in it, as a valuable remembrance, Stanley's photograph. At the sight of it our chronicler could not restrain a mocking laugh.

If there is anything for which the Arab or Swahili has by nature no appreciation, it is photographs. If his sight has not been trained by repeated trials to do so, he is quite unable to distinguish the person represented, however well known to him. Now that modern civilization has, among other important necessaries, introduced half a dozen photographers into the country, every native can acquire this faculty by staring at show-cases, and he even thinks it well worth while, if he can muster up the cost, to rescue his more or less handsome features from oblivion by having them imprinted on the dark plate. But that Tippu Tip, who in a rough nomad existence of twelve years had become a stranger even to the modest luxury of Zanzibar, should have the very slightest appreciation for the delicate attention of his Western friend, no sensible man could expect.

So he only felt surprised, and supposed when Stanley got home he would discharge the remainder of his debt and send the valuable presents promised.

After Tippu Tip had received these messages he needed a whole year to settle all his affairs in the country. As he expected to be away for a long time, he had to take care to fill the important posts with trustworthy men who combined prudence and energy with good will, and thus could well watch over his interests. In particular Nyongo Luteta, to whom he entrusted his affairs in Utetera, proved himself a very useful representative.

At last he set out, in company with his cousin Bwana Nzige. Large as was the host of carriers he took with him, it was not sufficient for the rapid transport of the boundless stores of ivory which he had been gathering together for years. Hence the following order of march was adopted: Tippu Tip went on ahead with the body of carriers, who took with them as many loads as they could possibly manage. After four hours' march he pitched his camp and sent the carriers back to his cousin, who remained behind with the unconveyed ivory. When the remainder reached Tippu Tip's camp next morning, he proceeded further in the same manner. As the distance had thus to be traversed by the carriers three times, of course much time was lost, and the march from Utetera to Lake Tanganyika, which without burdens can at a pinch be made in a month, occupied half a year.

Lake Tanganyika had been since the far-off time when our traveller had last crossed it the goal of many African explorers, and had by their zeal been brought to the closer knowledge of the West. In February, 1858, the English travellers Speke and Burton were the first Europeans to sight the great inland sea; but the first Westerners to navigate it were Stanley and Livingstone, in 1872, after the successful search for the latter in the interior of the Dark Continent. Four years later it was systematically circumnavigated by Stanley in the course of the crossing of Africa which we have described. Much had also been contributed to the exploration of the great sheet of water in 1873 by Cameron, and later on, between 1878 and 1880, by the travellers Hore, Thomson and Cambier, Bohm and Reichhardt.

Tippu Tip struck the lake at the port of Mtoa, which was known to him of old and used by all the caravans that trafficked with the West. By the busy stir which he found here he could judge how long he had been a stranger to the Eastern world. Where formerly only primitive dug-outs rocked on the waves, stately vessels, such as are to be seen in the Indian Ocean, now proudly spread their sails to the wind. Even some representatives of the Western lands, where thirty years before the very existence of the inland sea had been a fable, had established a permanent camp here in the heart of the Dark Continent. Close beside the Arab town from which the caravans started for the West on their man-destroying traffic, the English missionstation of Plymouth Rock looked out on the country from a low hill, like a bulwark of peace and herald of a new civilization. The manager of the station, Mr. Griffith, gave a friendly greeting to the Arab prince, who was probably well known to him by the accounts of returning caravans.

On the eastern shore, opposite Mtoa, and in good weather only one day's sail from it, lies the well-known Arab town of Ujiji. Here it was, as we have already seen, that on November 10, 1871, Stanley found Livingstone. He describes the Arab settlement as a flourishing commercial town, in the much-frequented market of which the tribes of the whole interior of Africa fixed their rendezvous. Wissmann, who in 1882 passed through it soon after our traveller, found that the town had fallen off greatly since Stanley's visit. Many houses stood empty, and their state of disrepair proclaimed that they had long been uninhabited. The population was composed partly of Arabs, with their numerous slaves, partly of free natives of the country. The Wajiji were exceedingly skilful navigators, and as such were much employed by the Arabs.

Though the latter formed the ruling class, the real autocrat of the town was a Swahili named Mwinyi Heri. He had been appointed governor by Seyyid Bargash, and, as the symbol of his power, proudly hoisted over his hut the red flag of the Sultan.

Ujiji was, however, still an important *entrepot*, where the products of the country were daily displayed for sale in large quantities, beside the wares of their native Zanzibar- fish, fruit, salt, butter, honey, slaves, ivory and cattle on the one side; on the other, samples of the wares that were brought by European ships to the shops of the Indians of Zanzibar. Glass beads, red or blue, were in use as payment for the humbler articles.

As a port Ujiji was not well chosen, as the shore is flat and unprotected, so that vessels have constantly to be drawn high and dry. At Wissmann's coming some forty dhows lay in the roadstead-a number never reached at a single port on the coast of German East Africa.

Tippu Tip halted for the present at Mtoa, but sent his cousin on to greet the Arabs living at Ujiji, to obtain water carriage, and to inquire into the possibility of continuing the march to Tabora. The country was, it must be said, in the highest degree unsafe for caravans, for a powerful native prince named Mirambo had for many years carried on a war of extermination with the Arabs.

We will pause for a moment to consider this interesting personality.

Mirambo was born about 1830 in Unyamwezi, where his grandfather, Mvura, was set up as Sultan of the small and poor district of Ugoa by Tippu Tip's grandfather, Juma bin Rajab. After Mvura's death an uncle of Mirambo's succeeded to the sultanate, while he himself was left to earn his living unaided; and in spite of his high family connections he adopted, like most of his compatriots, the calling, more lucrative than princely, of a *mpagasi* (carrier).

On the death of his uncle he became Sultan. He soon extended widely the borders of his hitherto insignificant dominion. With the help of the free-booting Wangoni he first conquered the neighbouring country of Uriankuru, which, together with Ujoa, he united in the sultanate called after him Urambo. By the plundering of many Arab caravans numerous rifles fell into his hands, with the aid of which he extended his influence westward almost to Lake Tanganyika, northwards to the Victoria Nyanza, and southwards to the sixth degree of latitude. His successes made such an impression that supernatural powers were everywhere attributed to him. it was said that he could fly, was invulnerable, and needed no sleep.

With the Arabs of Tabora he was at first on fairly peaceable terms. They reluctantly paid the *hongo* imposed on their caravans, and did not venture in their constant state of disunion to attempt anything against so dangerous a chieftain. At last, however, his encroachments seem to have grown excessive, and in the summer of 1871 it came to a sanguinary encounter between the two parties. Stanley* was just at that time the guest of the Arabs at Tabora, and took part in the conflict. He assigns as the cause of the war that Mirambo had demanded of a caravan marching to Ujiji an exceptionally high toll, and because difficulties were made about the payment, which was, however, at last made, he forbade all Safaris whatever to pass through his territories for the future. Tippu Tip declares that the quarrel broke out because Mirambo refused to hand over 200 slaves of the Arabs who had fled to his country.

At any rate, when Stanley arrived at Tabora the fury of the Arabs was boundless. The general anger was especially fanned by Khamis bin Abdullah el Barwani, an influential man who, in the course of long journeys, had grown used to bloody conflicts, and regarded it as a disgrace that his fellow-tribesmen there, among whom he had for some time made his home, allowed themselves to be so terrorized by a mere unbeliever.

After long deliberation, a force of 2,255 men, with 1,500 muskets, took the field

---

* *Cf.* 'How I found Livingstone,' chap. viii.

against Mirambo in the beginning of August, confident of victory. At the end of a week they returned to Tabora in wild flight. Mirambo had fallen on one of the divisions marching against him on the frontier of Uriankuru in the high grass, and destroyed it almost to a man. At the news of this disaster the remaining heroes also turned tail.

On the 22nd of the month Mirambo appeared in person before Tabora. Khamis bin Abdullah, the one brave man among the Arabs, went out against him; but his little force was surrounded by the superior forces of the native and annihilated. Mirambo then stormed some of the less well fortified *tembes*, burned down several houses, and looted a quantity of cattle and 200 elephant's tusks. Then he returned, well satisfied, to his own territory.

Since that time a regular guerilla warfare had been carried on between Mirambo and the Arabs. They had done each other as much damage as possible by plundering, as occasion presented itself; but the Arabs suffered the most, as their caravans could only get to the lake in fear and trembling by secret paths.

At the end of a fortnight Bwana Nzige returned with the news that the road to Tabora was difficult of passage owing to the enmity with Mirambo; but his compatriots at Ujiji begged Tippu Tip to come to them as soon as possible, to talk over in person the details of the further march. Tippu Tip determined to venture on the journey at all hazards. He intended to leave behind the greater portion of his ivory and take with him principally armed men, under whose protection he hoped to convey safely some 100 *frasilas*. From Tabora he would then send fresh armed bands to Ujiji to fetch the ivory left behind without risk.

At Ujiji he had intended to stay with the Vali, Mwinyi Heri; but an Arab named Mohammed bin Khalfan invited him to come to him, and Tippu Tip, after assuring himself that the chief official of the town would not take it badly accepted the invitation. This meeting with his as yet unknown compatriot was destined to have disastrous results to our hero, as the subsequent history will show. Rumalisa-such is the widely familiar sobriquet of his new friend-robbed Tippu Tip of a large portion of his fortune.

Soon after the arrival at Ujiji fresh intelligence came from Tabora to the effect that the road was now quiet. Tippu Tip thereupon altered his plan so as to take the whole of the ivory with him, and make for his father's town by the nearest way, vias Rwanda and Uvinza. He was joined by the Arab Salum bin Abdullah el Marhubi, who had been appointed by the Sultan administrator of the inheritance of Said bin Ali, who had died at Kassongo, and accordingly the far from inconsiderable stores of ivory of his friend had been handed over to him at Ujiji. Less than a day's march from that place our travellers found themselves already exposed to various hostilities on the part of the Warwanda. Salum, who had lagged somewhat behind with his men, was surprised by the Shensis and completely stripped. He with difficulty saved his bare life, and reached the camp late in the evening, in rags and bespattered with filth. Two of Tippu Tip's men who had ventured some way from the camp to fetch wood, were also killed. Next morning the natives ventured an open attack, but were repulsed.

Then Tippu Tip assumed the offensive. He constructed an entrenched camp, from which he made raids into the surrounding country. The very first day he had asked support of his countrymen at Ujiji, which soon arrived. With their assistance the whole country was soon devastated, and made so subject to the control of our hero that he was able to regard himself as at home and send for the whole of his ivory. After the lapse of some months his eldest son, Sef, visited him. He had been left behind as a small boy at Zanzibar, where he was brought up. Now he was eighteen years old, and had joined some business friends of his father's-the Arabs Salum bin Omar el Wardi and Said bin Habib el Afifi on their first trading trip into the interior. He brought a great number of Wanyamwezi with him, who were very welcome to Tippu Tip as carriers and enable him to convey a large portion of his ivory.

His fellow-tribesmen at Ujiji viewed his departure with regret. They had taken a delight in the expeditions under Tippu Tip's ever-victorious leadership, and were afraid that without the prestige of his dreaded name they would not be a match for the numerous Shensis. At their request he left them 140 guns, with the corresponding number of warriors by means of whom Rumalisa and Mwinyi Heri reckoned on holding in awe Rwanda and Uvinza. Tippu Tip, however, did this unwillingly, and seems not to have approved of the plans for further fighting. 'These people must always be making war,' he writes in reprobation.

His way through Uvinza was not a path of roses. The ruler there was the powerful Sultan Kasanura, who exacted heavy tolls from travellers. Besides, he carried off all the slaves he could lay hand on, and carriers who ventured away from the camp were inexorably killed.

Our hero would gladly have had recourse to arms in face of these outrages, but prudence restrained him, as he had a large train of carriers and but few fighting men, and defeat would have been likely and the loss of ivory irreparable. Postponing his plans of revenge to a future date, he put up with all these arbitrary acts, and at length, though heavily fleeced, reached Tabora in safety.

He halted at Itura, his wonted quarters. There, after long years, he saw his old father once more, and his step-brother, Mohammed bin Masoud, happened to be there also. 'The dancing, the killing of cattle, and the feasting lasted a fortnight. The merriment was extraordinary.

From Tabora Tippu Tip at once placed himself in communication again with the Sultan and his banker. In order to enable him to provide for the safe transport of his unconveyed ivory, he begged the former to send him a large quantity of powder. The answer came by return that the Sultan had pleasure in presenting him with twenty hundred-weight, which would reach him through the agency of Taria Topan.

As our hero, delighted at this prospect, was just about to return to Lake Tanganyika, there came an embassy from the dreaded Mirambo to old Mohammed bin Juma with offers of peace. He appealed to the fact that there had never been enmity between them. On the contrary, since the time of their fathers they had been united in the bonds of friendship. He, Mirambo, respected Mohammed as a father, as he had shown often enough. He had always given Mohammed credit for equally friendly sentiments, though he naturally could not give expression to them out of regard for the other Arabs, Mirambo's sworn enemies. Now he had heard that the son of his friend had difficulties with regard to the ivory left behind on Lake Tanganyika. He, Mirambo, would certainly put no hindrances in his way, and begged him to pass through his territory without fear. He was delighted to make the acquaintance of the far-travelled caravan leader.

Tippu Tip eagerly took advantage of this favourable disposition, and sent off messengers at once to assure Mirambo of his friendship. On reaching his town, however, they did not find the chief himself there-he had just started on a fresh expedition against the Sultan of Tabora. His brother, Mpanda Sharo, who had remained behind, received the envoys with all honour, and dismissed them with valuable presents.

The news that Mirambo was again on the warpath soon reached the Arabs at Tabora, but they did not know against whom he was marching, and racked their brains as to the object of his new hostilities.

Tippu Tip meanwhile had departed westwards. On the frontier of the Tabora territory messengers from his compatriots reached him warning him to go no further, as he might any moment happen upon Mirambo's bands. It was the ninth of the month El Hadj, the eve of the great Arab feast, which he, like all his countrymen, was in the habit of celebrating with great scrupulosity even in the most difficult situations. He replied quite calmly:

'To-day is the ninth of the month; to-morrow is the tenth of the month El Hadj. As soon as the feast has been kept I shall set out, and all things are in the hand of God, the Lord of Might. I cannot stay. It would cost me much money, and the carriers would also make difficulties for me, in order to get home again.'

In accordance with this programme, he started off after the feast, and encamped near the sources of the Wataturu, one of the few watering-places on this route, visited by every traveller. Here people were wont to provide themselves with the precious fluid sufficiently for the next few days, which led through districts where water was scarce. In the night a heavy torrent of rain broke over them quite unexpectedly, as it was the dry season. All the guns were wet, and there was reason to fear that the powder in them had become useless, so it was proposed to discharge them all and load afresh.

A tremendous volley rang out from 500 muskets, which thundered far and wide through the wilderness, and was heard by Mirambo's men, who were just marching towards the celebrated watering-place. He was returning from a successful expedition, and had no idea that Tippu Tip was near at hand. Nevertheless, he called out at once when he heard the thunder of innumerable guns: 'That must be Hamed bin Mohammed. No one can shoot like him.' In the hope that Tippu Tip's route would lead him past his camping-place, he remained there a day longer.

Tippu Tip, however, had as yet no news of the peaceful result of his mission, and therefore thought it more advisable to avoid for the present a meeting with the powerful chief. Continuing his march at greater speed, he came on many traces of Mirambo's column, and was therefore forced to take special precautions in advancing. Suddenly a fusillade was heard from the rear-guard. Two men were hit by bullets, and in the general confusion various loads went astray. As it turned out later, this was not a deliberate attack by Mirambo, but some of his men who had left the column to plunder had made a marauding attack on their own account, without knowing that the object of it was their master's friend Tippu Tip.

After a few further marches Tippu Tip reached Uvinza, where he now intended to take his revenge for the injury done him when marching through. He had beforehand warned Rumalisa to be ready to support him. How he settled accounts with his old enemy Kasanura we can learn best from his own narrative:

'We decided to declare war and attack the Sultan of Uvinza, Kasanura. He had settled on a river. There are five or six ditches there-half on one side and the other half on the other. His town is laid out exactly in the middle. It was strongly fortified and surrounded by a moat. Behind the first entrenchment a second was built, and inside long tree-trunks were planted. The intervening space between the entrenchments was filled up with sand, so that no bullets could penetrate. Towers with loopholes were also built. There was no point open to attack. But we did not know that the city was like that, and sent out men to attack it. They marched there, and passed the first and the second and the third ditch. The water rose to their belts or a trifle higher. When they advanced towards the *boma* the Wavinza in it remained quiet, but when they came quite near they were fired on with small shot, and the enemy sallied out and they were driven back, and many were killed. We asked those that came back: "How are things there?" They replied: "We have come back again, though you could hardly have hoped for it. The rest have all fallen." They came back in twos and threes, and by the evening forty-six men were missing who had fallen. Their guns were lost, and some even that escaped had thrown theirs away, to the number of thirty.

'We waited two days, and on the third I decided to start-ourselves, and our belongings, and our wives. We marched as far as the river and there pitched our tents. Next morning we passed the ditches, and they sallied out, and it came to a furious encounter between us, and they fell back to their fastness. Next day we crossed with our packs and our followers, and traversed all three ditches. Then we pitched our tents, but our camp had no entrenchment. They sallied out several times, but we drove them back, and they fled to their *boma*. Each time several men fell, both on their side and on our side. So we remained for several days, but their *boma* was not to be got at on account of its many defences.

'And they sent out men secretly to beg support of Mirambo, but he refused, saying: "Hamed bin Mohammed is my friend. I cannot help you." And he informed me of this. So a month and a half passed by, and the struggle became still more furious, but there was no getting at their *boma*. Mohammed bin Khalfan said to me: "Shall we not go into the moat and fight with them?" I answered him: "You understand nothing of war. You have never fought. He who goes into the moat does not come out again. It becomes his grave, and the attack is foiled." And I had a number of workmen with me-carpenters-to whom I said: "Make planks ready for me, but they must be of heavy wood." They went away and sent across ten boats, which were very large and of heavy timber. They dragged them to the spot and broke them up. So we got long planks. These planks we nailed together and made wheels underneath. Then we took this framework to the ditch and set up other planks on the top, so that those in the towers should not see the men inside the structure, and when they fired the bullets would only penetrate the wood a little way, but no men would be hurt. And we felled trees also to strengthen the structure. When we had done we went inside-we and the best of our slaves. While we were inside the men dragged the machine forwards, for it went on wheels. We had made loopholes in it also. The enemy came out and endeavoured to get at us, but could not. So at last we came down into the moat. Then tree-trunks were brought to build the *boma* still higher. The structure stood firm, and we worked till late in the night. When we were higher than their *boma*, no one could leave their *boma* any more. And inside the houses were built of grass. We set them alight during the night, and the people fled out of the town, and many were killed and some taken prisoners, and we set up another Sultan.'

Tippu Tip's delight at this victory was damped by the news that his old father had died at Tabora. At the same time, however, came from there the cheering intelligence that the powder presented by Seyyid Bargash had arrived meanwhile, and had already been sent on by Msabbah bin Niem, the newly-appointed Vali of the Lake Tanganyika district. Thus Tippu Tip found himself in a position to take with him all the ivory left behind on the lake within a measurable space of time.

At Ujiji he parted company with his old travelling companion, Mohammed bin Said. The latter felt a longing to return to the flesh-pots of Manyema, and our hero was not sorry to hand over to him his affairs in that country. He sent to all his subordinates letters instructing them for the future to acknowledge Bwana Nzige as their master, and give up all the ivory to him. Yet he made the stipulation that his friend before departing should await the arrival of the ammunition expected from Tabora.

When he himself was about to quit Ujiji, Rumalisa earnestly begged him to take him with him. In spite of his many raids in Uvinza, he had gathered no moss'; on the contrary, he had run, through the whole of a fortune entrusted to him by his kinsman Juma bin Abdallah. The latter, a friend of our traveller, had already several times requested him by letter to send him back either his property or Rumalisa's person.

Out of consideration for his cheated friend on the one hand, and on the other out of pity for Rumalisa's helplessness, Tippu Tip allowed himself to be persuaded to take him with him to the coast at his expense.

Many other Arabs had joined the caravan, which marched unmolested through the now subject Uvinza. Things did not go so well when they reached the neighbourhood of Usoki, where the old dread of Mirambo awoke in the Arabs once more. For years it had become a recognised thing that caravans no longer took the ordinary route through inhabited localities, but made their way through the desert by secret tracks, known only to the initiated. A special reputation as guide was enjoyed by a Mnwamwezi named Katutuvira. He knew every waterhole in the wilderness, and earned good money by guiding trading parties that were seeking to avoid Mirambo.

But although our travellers had secured the much-sought-for pathfinder, they ran straight into Mirambo's arms. Some careless carriers had strayed, as usual, from the watering-place, which was reached at noon. In their endeavours to find hokey in the bush, they ventured somewhat further from the camp than was advisable, and suddenly found themselves in face of the advance-guard of a force of the dreaded chief. Four were taken prisoners, and the rest fled back to the camp with the terrible news ' Mirambo is coming.' All preparations for defence were speedily made, but scarcely had they begun to drag thornbushes to the spot for a zareba, when the captives returned in good case and reported that they had parted on the best of terms from Mirambo's warriors. When these learned that they belonged to Tippu Tip, they at once treated them as friends, and told them their master had strictly forbidden them to harm him or his men. Soon after envoys came from Mirambo and exchanged greetings and presents with the Arabs. Next morning Tippu Tip saw the whole train pass; it was an imposing force on its return from a successful raid.

Without further adventure the traveller reached Tabora, where unhappily he did not find his aged father living. His stepmother, Nyaso, however, received him with all honour, and he, too, showed her all the respect due to the wife of his deceased father. Not long before his death the latter had laid her tenderly on Tippu Tip's breast with the touching words: 'Man knows not the hour of his death. If I die, look to thy mother, Nyaso, daughter of Fundi Kira, and that with both eyes, if thou wishest that I should be satisfied with thee.' And he had replied: 'If God will, she shall be even better off than in thy lifetime.'

Mohammed bin Masoud had meanwhile made himself useful by conveying all the ivory stored at Tabora to the coast. So there remained to be transported only what had just been brought from Lake Tanganyika. As it was just the season for tilling the fields, and carriers were not to be had, Tippu Tip determined for the present to proceed without loads and leave the care of the ivory to his brother.

His plans, however, were crossed by a fresh invitation from Mirambo. Either he was to come himself or send his son Sef on a visit. Tippu Tip determined on the latter, but encountered resistance from the Arabs at Tabora. They did not believe in the peaceful intentions of their old enemy, and prophesied that Sef would certainly be murdered, Tippu Tip answered them in his superior way: 'Then it does not matter.'

He had just then a large caravan ready to proceed to Ujiji. He now caused it to take the road to Urambo, and young Sef, richly provided with presents for the chief, joined it. His reception at Mirambo's town was, if we may believe the autobiography, a most brilliant one.

The Arabs were furious that Tippu Tip was so friendly towards their enemy. They were animated by a blind hatred against Mirambo, who had done them many an evil turn, and although peaceful intercourse would have been to their interest, they would not hear of a compromise with the insolent unbeliever. While they, like their fathers and brothers, had for years risked life and property in their feud with him, Tippu Tip had been attending to his selfish interests in Manyema. He knew nothing of the righteous hatred which the loss of kinsmen who had fallen in war, the plundering of rich convoys, and the murder of numberless slaves, had nourished in their hearts. Just because it suited him they were to forego their most precious prize-revenge! Well, they were much obliged for the offer of a peace which they did not want, and they recoiled from no means of ruining the prospects of conciliation.

After having tried in vain to hold Sef and his people back from the trip by gloomy prognostications, they devised a frightful snare to entice him and his caravan to destruction.

They sent ten Wanyamwezi disguised as men of the coast to Mirambo, informing him that Seyyid Bargash had sent a great army from the coast to the support of the Arabs, and would shortly attack him with superior numbers; they, the ten men, had escaped on the road to give him timely warning. Their whole bearing and dress were calculated to obtain credence. 'They looked like people who had come from a journey.'

The Arabs had hoped that Mirambo, as soon as he received this news, would at once seize young Sef, and if he did not kill him, at least keep him so long as a hostage that a subsequent reconciliation would be impossible. But he did not allow himself to be taken in so easily. He told Tippu Tip's son what had been secretly alleged, but added that he did not believe the story. Far from doing his guests any harm, all he thought of was that no unpleasantness should result to them from the stories told. He begged Sef to get the other Arabs to depart with their caravans, for as soon as the story became further known, their Wanyamwezi would get frightened and return to Tabora; then they would have no more carriers and would suffer great losses.

The Arabs acted on the suggestion, and Sef too, some days later, returned with valuable presents to his native town.

In the days when Sef paid Mirambo this memorable visit, Wissmann, then on his way from the West Coast, was also a guest of the dreaded chief. He depicts* Mirambo as a man of tall and sinewy build, placid, attractive features, and gentle speech. His exterior and bearing gave no hint that he was the hero before whom for ten years past hundreds of Arabs and thousands of natives had trembled. Mirambo very hospitably offered the German traveller entertainment, and showed him with pride his extensive arsenal, in which many guns, great quantities of powder, and innumerable spears, bows, and arrows were stored. We also learn from Wissmann the date when Sef made his entry-August 31, 1882. The European traveller describes Tippu Tip's son as a young man of twenty with a chivalrous bearing. His handsome exterior was spoiled by a furtive glance, and he certainly afterwards afforded Wissmann proofs of a spiteful disposition. Tippu Tip clung with especial affection to this his eldest son, and never quite got over his early death, of which we shall hear later.

Of the exact circumstances under which Tippu Tip's mission was sent Wissmann gives a somewhat different account. He says the desire to make peace originated with our hero, who, as the Uvinza route was made precarious in consequence of Mirambo's constant raids, desired to secure a road through his territory for his caravans of costly goods. He also says that Mirambo posed as benefactor towards Sef, and received the son of the famous traveller politely, it is true, but treated him throughout as a suppliant.

It is hardly doing an injustice to the future Imperial Commissioner if one ventures to doubt whether at that time, when he came from the West as a perfect stranger, he had a just appreciation of the state of affairs. There is much in favour of Tippu Tip's statement that Mirambo desired peace. He had, as Wissmann himself acknowledges, great stores of ivory, which he could not turn to account against the will of the Arabs. Even if he succeeded by means of his military superiority in carrying his caravans through the forbidden region of the Tabora people, it was still necessary to convey the ivory to the purchaser on

---

*Wissmann, 'Unter deutscher Flagge quer durch Afrika,' chap. xiii. (Berlin, 1899).

the coast. Now, the natural ally of the Tabora Arabs was their Sultan at Zanzibar. He could at any time lay an embargo on the treasures that had safely reached the sea as a war indemnity for his subjects, and then all the trouble of sending the convoys so far would be wasted.

Wissmann himself mentions later on that Mirambo was thoroughly desirous of making peace with Seyyid Bargash. And to whom could he have applied rather than Tippu Tip, with whom he was connected by family traditions, who cherished no personal grudge against him, as he had been absent during the principal conflicts, and who, having regard to the importance of his caravans, could only profit from peaceful relations? Perhaps Wissmann attached too much significance to the official dignity with which the powerful Sultan met the young Arab. In any case, it was to the interest of both to make peace, and it was only natural that both did their best finally to attain it.

Wissmann also speaks of the legend regarding the army supposed to have been sent by Seyyid Bargash, though in a somewhat altered form.

He learned from Sef that his father meant to proceed very shortly to Zanzibar. As he had but a few men with him, and on the way to Lake Tanganyika had learned to his cost to what risks an insufficiently protected caravan was exposed, he decided to join the Arab chief on his further march to the coast.

On September 5 he reached Tabora, and drew up at the Catholic mission-house, a large *tembe* with a roomy veranda. The year before the White Fathers of the Algerian Mission had made their abode here, and had already left their mark on the country round.

Wissmann here had the opportunity of observing that, in contradistinction to the Evangelical missions, which chiefly devoted themselves to doctrinal efforts, the Catholics attached more importance to practical training in civilization. With but narrow means at their disposal, they had installed themselves admirably. Gardening, agriculture, and cattle-breeding flourished under their guidance. He was bidden welcome with the cheering hospitality usual in the wilds.

Two days later he paid Tippu Tip-to whom he handed a letter of recommendation from his son-a visit in his town of Ituru. He describes him graphically as 'a man of about forty- five and quite black in complexion, although his father was a pure Arab. Somewhat stout, he is yet very quick in his movements, graceful and polite, decided in his gestures, yet has often, like his son, a touch of watchfulness and furtiveness, and seems to be fond of mocking.'

This fondness for mockery, which at once struck Wissmann during his short visit, is indeed a characteristic of our hero which he retained till his old age. The statement that his father was a pure Arab is erroneous, as may be remembered from the second chapter.

Wissmann then told him about his journey, during which he had often come in contact with Tippu Tip's people, and everywhere been well treated by them. Then he expressed the wish that the sheikh would take him with him to the coast, and advance him the articles necessary for the journey. Tippu Tip agreed to this, and September 27 was fixed as the day for setting out together.

Well armed as the caravan was, yet it could not evade the numerous attempts at extortion on the part of the natives at Ugogo. There was a great drought in the country, and the few waterholes were jealously watched, the use of them not being conceded until after the payment of a considerable *hongo*. Unluckily also, the small-pox broke out in the convoy, claiming several victims daily, and forcing its leader to be exceptionally compliant.

Both travellers speak of these mishaps, Tippu Tip using the opportunity to present himself again as an angel of unselfishness. He says that the Wagogo only meant their demands for *hongo* for the Christian, but that, in order to spare Wissmann unpleasantness, he paid it all, without parley, out of his own pocket.

After a last wretched march through the cheerless Marenga Mkali, Mpapwa was reached at the end of October. Wissmann, who had gone on ahead with a small body, got there first, unmolested. Tippu Tip's caravan was surprised on the way by robbers, and suffered considerable losses in goods and lives. At Mpapwa their ways parted. Wissmann took the north road by Mamboge, and reached the coast near Saadani on November 15. He had thus, as he proudly boasts at the end of his book of travels, brought to a glorious conclusion the first crossing of the continent under the German flag. He was, moreover, the first man to make, from west to east, the journey already accomplished by Cameron and Stanley. And if anything goes to justify a biography of Tippu Tip it may well be the fact that he was the faithful guide, and had no small share in the success of these three pioneers in the crossing of Africa.

Jahazi sailing

Boats in Zanzibar Habour

CHAPTER XI

FRESH JOURNEY TO STANLEY FALLS

'Mene, mene, tekel, upharsin.'-DAN. v. 25.

Tippu Tip marched through Usagara to Bagamoyo, where he deposited his loads with the then agent of Taria Topan, the Indian Jan Mohammed Hansraj, who afterwards attained to wealth and high position in Zanzibar. That same day he started in a dhow for Zanzibar, and reached his home on the 9th of Mohurram, 1300 (November 22,1882). Although he did not land till nearly ten in the evening, he at once sought out his creditor, who knew already from Rumalisa, who had been sent on before, that Tippu Tip would follow directly. The Indian surprised him by the question whether he felt inclined to become Vali of Tabora, as the former Viceroy, Abdullah bin Nasib, had been recalled. Our traveller replied with a smile that he was King of a far larger country than the whole of Tabora, and was in a position to keep several Valis on his own account. Taria answered that Seyyid certainly entertained the idea of offering him the post at Tabora, and would feel greatly humiliated in his pride as Sultan if Tippu met the offer with a curt refusal; he must at least make a show of considering the proposal.

Next morning he again called on Taria, and found there a Belgian, who proposed to him to undertake a journey with him to Manyema. He, the Belgian, would supply guns and ammunition, while Tippu Tip was to find the necessary carriers. The proceeds of the journey were to be divided equally. Tippu Tip replied that he was a subject of the Sultan of Zanzibar, to whom, as a matter of course, his other territories were subject; if the latter gave his consent he would think the matter over. The Belgian represented to him, on the contrary, that he was sole ruler in Manyemaland, and the Sultan had no authority over him. Tippu Tip, however, persisted that he could undertake nothing without the Sultan's sanction.

That same morning he paid his visit to Seyyid Bargash, whose acquaintance he had not yet made. He had much to tell him about his successes in West Africa, and finally reported also the proposal of the Belgian. Bargash thereupon answered that he had really had it in his mind to make him Vali of Tabora, but from what he heard of his influence in Manyemaland and the plans of the European, he considered it more advisable that Tippu Tip should return speedily to his dominions, so as not to leave them a prey to the desires of the Western traveller. Tippu Tip begged for a respite, at least until the whole of his ivory had arrived from Tabora, but the Sultan pressed for a speedy departure.

However, our hero soon found excuses enough, with the usual Arab faculty of procrastination, to stay a considerable time at Zanzibar.

In the first place, Wissmann arrived, some days later, and had to be reckoned with. Tippu Tip says he only charged him for the goods advanced at cost price, and said nothing about the tolls paid for him at Ugogo.

Our traveller had also to hold consultations with the British Consul-General, his old acquaintances Sir John Kirk. He was particularly interested in the state of affairs at Ugogo, whose inhabitants had already given rise to many complaints by the systematic extortions they practised on passing caravans. He proposed to Tippu Tip to advise means, in concert with Seyyid Bargash, to bring the country wholly under his control. If the Sultan had taken this hint-if, as easily might have been done at that time, he had secured the roads to Ugogo by adequate military posts, and thrown large bodies of troops into the country-he would have been just in time to avert the loss of his great possessions in Africa. When, two years later, the chiefs of the districts lying between Ugogo and the coast submitted to the German Protectorate, the Sultan's protest passed unnoticed, because he could not prove that he had ever exercised substantive rights of sovereignty in those districts.

But Seyyid Bargash always had much less inclination for the extension of his political influence than for commercial undertakings. This observation was made at this very time by Wissmann when, on reaching Zanzibar, he duly paid his visit to the Sultan. Quite uneducated, as all the Oman Arabs still are, he had no conception of the vast tracts which his subjects had explored and subjugated in his name; and when Wissmann told him of the many countries through which he himself had passed, the only question that interested him was whether there was much gold and silver there. When he replied in the negative and could not even give satisfactory information as to the presence of coal, the interest of the Sultan was at an end. No other points of view existed for him.

Now his thoughts were only concentrated on the commercial opening-up of the districts extolled by Tippu Tip as rich in ivory and slaves, and he endeavoured, disregarding the political necessity of keeping the route to them open under all circumstances, first and foremost to secure a monopoly of trade for his subjects in the new regions.

In accordance with the Sultan's plenary powers at that time, he promulgated a decree, mainly directed against the Belgian, that no one should enlist carriers until Hamed bin Mohammed was sufficiently supplied. Taria was once more made to open an unlimited credit for him, and this time, after the first speculation had turned out so well, and Tippu Tip been so successful, probably was not unwilling to do so. Personally the Sultan heaped many tokens of his favour on the famous traveller. He presented him with 2,000 rupees in cash, besides rich stuffs and other things that delight the heart of the Oriental-fragrant perfumes, richly-adorned weapons, a gold watch, and a diamond ring.

On this fresh journey Tippu Tip took with him his newly-acquired friend Rumalisa. He had, indeed, intended to trade on his own account, but could not (as the autobiographer spitefully insists, in view of the enmity that afterwards arose between them) get anyone to lend him a farthing. Rumalisa's brother Nasor was also taken as a companion.

At Tabora our hero found letters from his cousin Bwana Nzige. He complained that the people in Manyema had become refractory, and that he felt powerless against them. If Tippu Tip did not come very quickly, he would expose himself to heavy losses, for much ivory lay ready for him.

Tippu Tip at once decided to march on, but could get no carriers at Tabora, as it was just harvest time. In his need he applied to Mirambo, who at once, like a true friend, sent him 200 men. Tippu Tip armed them and set off. His merchandise, to the value of 80,000 dollars, he left to the care of Rumalisa, who was to collect more carriers and then to follow.

As our hero, being sure of Mirambo's friendship, meant to take the shorter road through his country the Arabs again endeavoured to sow discord between them. They made out to Tippu Tip that he would certainly be attacked by Mirambo, and tried to persuade the latter that he was coming to make war on him. But once more their slanders failed. Tippu Tip was received with all honour, and Mirambo again requested him to intercede that he might secure final peace with Seyyid Bargash. He reported that he had on a previous occasion sent the Sultan a great supply of ivory, but the present had been declined; now he meant again to send him forty tusks, and Tippu Tip must try to convince him of the sincerity of his peaceful intentions.

Tippu Tip parted from his host on the best of terms, and on the 29th Rajeb, 1300 (beginning of June, 1883), reached the Arab settlement of Kwa Kassongo. Next day he visited his friends at Nyangwe.

After a short stay he continued his march to Sultan Lusuna, with whose help he got together a large force. With the energy characteristic of him, he soon restored order throughout his territories. While he was engaged in setting up new Valis, a letter reached him from old Juma Mericano, who was in great distress in a country north-west of the Lomami, the Sultan of which, Kassongo Karambo, had falsely persuaded him that he could do excellent business in ivory there. When he got there it turned out that the ruler had simply intended to cheat the stranger out of his merchandise. He forbade his subjects to sell ivory direct to the Arab; Juma had to buy it all from the Sultan himself at high prices, and did not receive permission to leave the country till he had found a purchaser for all his goods.

But matters were brought to a crisis by the fact that the Sultan had been audacious enough to claim as his property several tusks of Tippu Tip's that had been handed over to Juma. This gave our friend the desired excuse for extending his authority to this country.

On the way there he did some advantageous strokes of business at Ukosi. How he went about the work he does not say in his autobiography, only he remarks, significantly enough, that as soon as he approached all the Shensis ran away and gave him the new sobriquet of Mkangwansara. The meaning of this title is said to have been 'He is afraid of nothing, or only fears that he and his men not find enough provisions.'

The country was rich in copper. In six days he acquired 700 *frasilas*. He then marched in a northerly direction through thickly populated localities, and at length reached the capital of Kassongo, Karombo. There he found some 3,000 adults, one and all drunk. He only came across one Moslem, a young man from the coast named Musa, His friend Juma was among the drunken, for which reason our traveller does not reckon him as a co-religionist. Painfully the old sinner dragged himself to the *barasa* of his house to welcome his deliverer. But the greeting came to an abrupt conclusion by Juma at once falling into a leaden sleep. When his renegade friend had become sober next morning, Tippu Tip held a most categorical palaver with the Sultan, which ended in his not only handing over all the goods he had stolen, but giving him ten tusks of ivory in addition as compensation.

Tippu Tip's task was thus completed. Juma Mericano, however, who had still various items of business on hand, could not get away so quickly. He begged his friend to go on alone for the present, but first to exert all his influence that no hindrances might be placed in the way of his departure later on.

When this had also been satisfactorily arranged, Tippu Tip got under way. During his return march he had opportunities for remarkable studies in civilization. In almost every place he came across people with ears and noses cut off. These mutilations had been inflicted on them by Rungu Kabare, a Sultan who had once held sway over the whole of Urua. In order to give visible expression to his power he had, according to justice or caprice, treated his subjects in this way. He had held absolute sway far away to the east, and would, Tippu Tip thinks, have made even Ujiji and Tabora unsafe, but that the great Lake Tanganyika checked his advance.

In his expeditions he used his mutilated subjects as bogies. He placed them in the foremost ranks, and as soon as the enemy caught sight of the earless and noseless *promachi*, they were so stricken with panic that they promptly took to flight.

After Rungu Kabare's death, his son Kassongo Rushie succeeded him; but he was unable to maintain the power of his father. Many disputes arose between the various descendants, which soon split up the once powerful kingdom.

Tippu Tip passed through the province of Ngongo, who remained, as before, a loyal and freelypaying subject of his master, back to Nyangwe. He only stayed there a month, and then marched on down-stream to the so-called Stanley Falls, where, as their most easterly *point d'appui*, the International Congo Company had meanwhile established a fortified station.

It will not be out of place to give here a short sketch of the events which led to the founding of the independent Congo State.

In September, 1876, the King of the Belgians summoned an 'International Conference to consider the means for the systematic exploration of Africa,' at Brussels. To this meeting the presidents of all the larger geographical societies were invited, and representatives of almost all the European States attended it. The King, who opened the Conference in person at his palace, proposed to form an International Society for the Exploration and Civilization, of Central Africa. The proposal was received with enthusiasm, and in connection with the Association Internationale Africaine thus created, numerous national committees were formed in the States concerned, with the object of concentrating the colonial aspirations of the various countries, and advancing them in accordance with the principles adopted by the International Union. The ideals aimed at were scientific exploration on a harmonious plan, the opening of ways of communication by which trade and civilization might penetrate into the interior, and the devising of means for the suppression of slavery. For the carrying out of these objects stations were as far as possible to be founded, which were to make scientific observation of the tracts within their reach, and afford hospitality to passing travellers.

FRESH JOURNEY TO STANLEY FALLS

The widespread interest which the Dark Continent had for some time excited developed into general enthusiasm when, in August, 1877, Stanley returned from his eventful crossing of Africa, and related marvellous stories of the alleged wealth of the tracts he had passed through. After his unexampled success he seemed the right man for the objects of the Association Internationale Africaine.

After his attempt to exploit commercially the countries he had discovered with the help of English capital had been wrecked by the backwardness of the capitalists, who, not satisfied with brilliant descriptions, demanded material guarantees, Stanley in 1878 began negotiations in Brussels. These led to the foundation, under the presidency of King Leopold, of a Comité d'Études du Haut Congo, under the auspices of which Stanley took charge of a splendidly equipped expedition. The outfit, which included a steamboat of 25 tons, four launches, and a large number of boats and lighters, was despatched by special steamer to the mouth of the Congo, while Stanley himself proceeded to Zanzibar to recruit the necessary men there.

On August 21, 1879, the expedition started up the Congo; but, as is often the case, the successful explorer did not prove a skilful organizer. True, a number of stations were established in the region of the lower Congo, but all these undertakings swallowed up great sums of money, and not the slightest trace was to be found on the spot of the stores of wealth which the country was said to possess. Moreover, the ideal aims of the Association Internationale, under whose banner the enterprise had come into existence, were not furthered in any visible way.

People at Brussels were already beginning to get very impatient when Stanley succeeded once more, by a personal sojourn in Belgium, in creating a feeling in favour of his mission, and though all his very extensive demands were not acceded to, yet very ample means were once more placed at his disposal.

At the end of 1882 he returned to the Congo. Ideal aspirations had ceased to produce any effect, and commercial enterprises for the present promised no result; so, in order to have something to show the wondering world, the preponderance was transferred to political acquisitions. Rights of sovereignty were acquired from the various chiefs, and the newly-created stations sprang like mushrooms from the soil. Forty of them were to be counted as far as the Stanley Falls. Their establishment had, it is true, cost £600,000, and after a short time all but a few of them were given up.

In the middle of 1884 Stanley again returned to Europe, and was replaced in the conduct of the Belgian enterprises by the English Colonel Sir Francis de Winton.

Soon afterwards the districts acquired in Central Africa received their political status. They were formed into the Congo Free State (État Indepéndant du Congo). King Leopold II, with the assent of the Belgian Chambers, became the head of a new political entity, which was solemnly proclaimed at Bwana on July 13, 1885.

Shortly before the so-called Congo Conference had sat at Berlin, and between November 15, 1884 and February 26, 1885, had discussed general ordinances regulating the freedom of trade in the Congo basin and the surrounding districts, the limitation of the slave trade, the neutrality of the free trade sphere, navigation on the Congo and Niger, as also the principles of future acquisitions of territory in Africa.

The furthest station established by the Belgians was, as we have said, Stanley Falls, which Tippu Tip now visited. From this point he sent out twenty large caravans to travel through the country, which was already further opened up. Most of these met with success, but the largest, under the Arab Salum bin Mohammed, was almost entirely wiped out. It went up the Aruwimi River, and there, while making itself at home in a deserted township, was surprised by the inhabitants returning by night, and was slaughtered and devoured almost to a man. This disastrous adventure was, as we shall see, to have a momentous sequel in the future history of our hero.

While Tippu Tip remained in these districts, which were daily falling more and more completely under Belgian rule, he received from Seyyid Bargash letters urging him to use every means in his power to keep the country under his influence. Tippu Tip replied that he himself was powerless without weapons and ammunition; if the Sultan wished him to do his best for him, he must first supply him with the necessary material. There upon Bargash called him back to talk over the situation in Manyemaland with him in person.

CHAPTER XII

RETURN HOME

'Prophets right and prophets left,
The worldling in the middle.'
GOETHE : *Dinner at Coblenz.*

Tippu Tip quickly settled his outstanding affairs, and started for Lake Tanganyika with a fresh store of ivory-900 *frasilas*, as he says. On the way messengers reached him from Rumalisa with no very edifying news. There was war at Uvinza, and Tippu Tip's merchandise, which represented a considerable capital, was in danger of being wholly lost if he could not at once place a large body of troops at Rumalisa's disposal. Acting on this advice, our hero sent 500 warriors, armed with guns, on ahead in all haste, and followed himself by forced marches. At Ujiji he found Rumalisa, to whom he gave further instructions for the conflict. Then he marched away to Tabora, reaching the town of his fathers in September, 1886.

Here, too, in spite of the short time he had spent beyond Lake Tanganyika, he found many things changed, to the disadvantage of his compatriots. If the Belgians on the west had seriously curtailed the Arab influence, on the east the Germans were threatening more and more to force backwards the Oriental sphere of power.

On April 3, 1884, the Society for German Colonization had been founded at Berlin, and at the end of the same year Dr. Peters had, under its orders, started on his famous flag-hoisting journey, which ended in the peaceful subjugation of the territories of Useguha, Nguru, Usegara, and Ukami. On February 27, 1885, the Emperor, William I, sanctioned the acquisition of the new districts by the issue of a charter. On April 25 Sultan Bargash was officially informed of the fact, and at once raised a protest at Berlin by telegraph. He insisted that the chiefs had had no right to alienate the districts acquired by Germany, for these-so ended the very sharply worded protest-belonged to him 'since the days of his fathers.'

The claims of the Sultan were, naturally, not acknowledged by the German Foreign Office. He had certainly exercised no effective rights of sovereignty over the ceded territories. It is sufficiently demonstrated by what has gone before that the Arabs who journeyed into the interior were habitually regarded by the natives as enemies. Almost everywhere our hero had to force a passage or purchase it by heavy payments, regulated by the caprice of the various chiefs. If the natives dealt so with the subjects of the Sultan of Zanzibar, it was quite plain that they did not fear his power, still less acknowledge his sovereignty.

That the Sultan had small military posts here and there can scarcely be taken into account. They were like oases in the desert, and their influence did not extend beyond the range of their guns. But even the few places where there were large colonies of Arabs, with Valis appointed by the Sultan, cannot be regarded as belonging to Zanzibar. As the conflicts round Tabora teach us, such Valis had no authority over the neighbouring natives; it only extended to the Arabs and people of the coast who lived near them. They were, in modern phraseology Consuls of the Sultan, invested with jurisdiction to a certain extent, but with this drawback-that their *exequatur* was only respected by the local rulers as long as it brought them advantage.

In order to break down the resistance of the Sultan to the German acquisitions, a strong squadron was sent in June to Zanzibar, and anchored menacingly before his palace. On August 14 Seyyid Bargash recognised the cession of the territories, and was clearly glad, in face of this display of force by the German Empire, that his whole country was not annexed. As a pendant to these proceedings, negotiations were entered on with England concerning the further development of West African affairs. These resulted, on November 1, 1886, in the London Convention, which formed the first international basis for German colonial aspirations. The Sultan was acknowledged as Suzerain over the islands of Zanzibar, Pemba, Lamu, and Mafia, and a belt on the coast ten miles broad, from the Rovuma to Kipini. Germany acceded to an agreement concluded between England and France in 1882, by which the independence of the Sultan was guaranteed. In order to make accessible by sea the new acquisitions of the colonizing association-which had meanwhile been transformed into the German East African Company-England promised its good offices to induce the Sultan to lease to it the customs harbours of Dar-es-salaam and Pangani. The joint use of the former had already been conceded to the Company in September, 1885. In addition to this, Germany and England agreed to delimit shortly their respective spheres of influence in the treaty districts. As a supplement to this treaty, Bargash let himself be persuaded in 1887 to farm the whole of the Customs on the coast to the German Company. A formal treaty regulating the details was signed in April, 1888, by his successor and brother, Khalifa.

The economic opening up of the East Coast territories went hand-in-hand with their political conquest. As long ago as the beginning of the nineteenth century American whale-fishers had come in contact with Zanzibar, and since 1830 the American firm of John Bertram had been firmly established there. It sent sailing vessels from time to time to the Indian Ocean, and exchanged Western clothing materials for coffee in Arabia, and for ivory, rubber, and cloves in the East African capital. Soon afterwards the Hamburg firm of O'Swald also set up at Zanzibar. Till then the West Coast had been its sphere of action, but in 1846 it sent a ship to the East Coast to obtain the cowrie-shells, which were current there as money. The favourable conditions of trade found to prevail there encouraged the firm to establish a permanent settlement. Near the Custom-house it acquired a piece of land, on which it erected a house, which still counts among the finest and most convenient buildings in the town. In 1859 the Hanse Towns established at Zanzibar a Consulate, the management of which was entrusted to the firm. After the consular representation was

RETURN HOME

taken over, first by the North German Confederation and later by the German Empire, the post was held by the head of the firm for the time being till 1884, when a regular German Consulate was created.

In the sixties an employee who was leaving the firm of O'Swald founded a rival establishment for the Hamburg house of Hansing and Co., while in 1874 the great ivory firm of H. A. Meyer set up a branch at Zanzibar. While the two first-named carried on business on the spot, the professional activity of the latter gradually necessitated getting into touch with the interior. Countries really rich in ivory were even then scarcely to be found on this side of Lake Tanganyika. The nearest good market was at Tabora, where, beside the tusks of the elephants killed in the country, much of the ivory obtained in Manyema was to be bought. The firm in July and August sent two representatives there, named Harders and Töppen, amply supplied with merchandise. They reached their destination at the end of the year, and at once encountered the greatest difficulties. The Arabs, as a matter of course, viewed with distrust the foreign element which desired to intrude into their midst. While the permanent society of the unbelievers was distasteful to them, the competition of the strangers was also to be dreaded. They worked with proper and reliable means, paid cash, and might, if left alone, end in attracting all the custom. Moreover, they were in a position to observe many Arab tricks, which, if reported on the coast, must create bad blood there. That the throne of their Sultan at Zanzibar no longer stood firm, and the accursed Franks, with their ships of war, had lately made a great display there, was not, of course, unknown to the Tabora people, thanks to their busy intercourse with the home country. Besides, of late so many strangers were going about the country, of whom no one knew rightly what they wanted. Formerly they had only laughed at the crazy fellows in tattered clothes who followed the courses of rivers of no importance, or climbed high mountains without getting any advantage thereby. But by degrees it seemed as if there was some tangible support behind these Westerners, and now that even the powerful Sultan of Zanzibar began to be subservient to them the matter was getting serious. So prudence was advisable. Open violence is contrary to the Oriental character as long as other means are at command. It is quite possible to keep an amiable countenance and harass one's enemies well at the same time. In East African legal affairs *dasturi* plays a great part: no Papal dogma is so infallible; and it is a part of *dasturi*, and a leading one, to give presents everywhere. Those who are unaware of this fact must be told of it.

So the Vali of Tabora, a man of noble birth, named Zid bin Juma, of course took good care duly to instruct the poor ignorant strangers. Leave to settle in Tabora was not refused, but they must make him presents for it; the purchase of ivory was allowed them, but in return they must bestow on the representative of the Sultan under whose protection they lived such a part of their merchandise as seemed suitable.

As a matter of course, too, they must show their gratitude to the ruler of the country for the hospitality afforded them. Mkasiva had died in the meantime, and his son Sike reigned in his stead, who, being of a covetous nature, liked to work hand-in-hand with the Arabs to extort as much as possible from the strangers. Thus in six weeks goods to the value of some 7,000 marks were wheedled out of the newcomers with an affable smile, or in case of refusal with alarming threats. If the Vali wanted anything he made the needs of the Sultan his excuse, while the Sultan in turn sheltered himself behind the Vali when he was in an acquisitive humour.

As, owing to these one-sided proofs of friendship, but little business could be done for the firm, in March, 1886, Töppen started for the coast to seek the intervention of the German Consulate-General in getting the Sultan to alter the *dasturi* practised by his subjects; but he fell ill from sunstroke, and so his arrival at Zanzibar was delayed. But as previous complaints as to the oppression of the agents at Tabora had already reached him, the Sultan indited various letters of advice to the Vali and Sike. These were despatched by a new representative of the firm, Giesecke, who was sent to Tabora in the early part of 1886. On the way he received the sad news that Harders had died of fever. A French traveller, Révoil, had been with him at the time of his death, and had meant to hold out in Tabora until a fresh agent of the firm appeared, to whom he might hand over the stock, of which he had taken charge in the meantime. His health forced him, however, to leave before this. He made out in the presence of witnesses a careful inventory of the Meyers' property, which was afterwards delivered to Giesecke. The goods intended for exchange proved to be intact, but it was found that forty tusks, of a value of some 14,000 marks, had been abstracted. The Arab Mohammed bin Kasum was subsequently unmasked as the perpetrator of the theft. He had undermined the approach to the Meyers' *tembe*, and carried off the ivory through the opening. This is a favourite method of burglary in East Africa.

The Sultan's letters of advice were of very little use-in fact, Sike, emboldened by the attitude of the Arabs, continued his attempts at extortion more shamelessly than ever. Even the permission to bury the deceased Harders in Taboran soil had to be bought by Giesecke at the cost of some 300 marks.

In addition to all this chicanery, on May 27, soon after his arrival, an attempt was made on Giesecke's life. While he was sitting in his room one evening he was fired at through the window, and the large bullets with which the gun was loaded struck the wall a short distance from his head.

The firm, in consequence, decided to give up the settlement at Tabora; but while they were debating as to the most advantageous way of conveying the existing stock to the coast a second murderous attack on Giesecke was perpetrated, which cost him his life. At the time when this happened Tippu Tip had just reached Tabora, and from this moment we can again follow his memoranda at first hand.

He begins by recording how Giesecke told him of his trouble as to the intrigues of the Arabs, the purloining of the ivory, and the first attempt on himself. He personally examined the place where the bullets had entered the wall, and on measuring found that the space between their marks and the place where Giesecke had sat was only an inch. Tippu Tip urged Giesecke to make the journey to the coast under his protection, and the offer was gratefully accepted.

He then narrates that he met yet another European at Tabora, who had passed the Khartoum to Wadelai, seen Emin Pasha, and then proceeded to Uganda. This was the Russian Dr Junker. This well-known traveller, born at Moscow in 1840, had already made two expeditions to the Southern Nile regions, in 1873 and 1876, and since 1879 had been engaged in exploring the sources of that river. He had, as Tippu Tip quite correctly states,

RETURN HOME

come across the well-known Emin Bey at Lado. Owing to the Mahdist rising, of which we shall have to speak again later on, his return by the northern route had been cut off. His brother, who lived in Russia and feared for his life, had sent out an expedition to his relief in 1884 under the German traveller Dr. Fischer. But he had to turn back without effecting his purpose, owing to the hostile action of King Mwanga of Uganda. Junker, however, succeeded in forcing his way for himself. Early in 1886 he started from Wadelai, and in the beginning of September of that year reached Unyanyembe. He took up his residence at the English mission-station of Ujui, not far from Tabora. Here he learnt that Tippu Tip would arrive in a few days and continue his march to the coast without stopping. He naturally wished, in view of the prevailing insecurity, to seize the opportunity to continue his journey under the protection of the powerful caravan leader.

To be sure, he had to pay dearly for this honour. From diaries left behind by Giesecke we learn that Junker paid Tippu Tip for carriers supplied by him the sum of 1,500 dollars. The usual tariff for a carrier from Tabora to the coast was at that time from 10 to 12 dollars, or at most 18 dollars, a total in round numbers of 700 dollars. The excess of 800 dollars was agreed on as a sort of life insurance, payable on the safe delivery of Junker at Zanzibar.

Tippu Tip did not wish to stay longer than necessary at Tabora, and so it was agreed to make ready for departure with all speed, and start at the end of September. In the interval the travellers pitched their camp in Ituru, the quarter where their protectors lived. There, in the night of the 27th, the fatal attempt on the unfortunate Giesecke was made. As Junker sat reading in his tent towards eleven in the evening he was suddenly startled by shots close at hand. At the same moment he heard pitiful calls for help from Giesecke's tent, only twenty paces away. Hastening there at once, he found the young merchant mortally wounded. He remained all night with him, while Tippu Tip, who had speedily come to the scene at the news of the disaster, sent messengers to the Catholic mission-station at Kiparapara to beg for further assistance. Then the Arab chief, wounded to the quick by this treacherous attack in his own camp, proceeded straight to Tabora to call the Vali Zid bin Juma to account for the breach of the peace. As to what followed we had best listen to his own descriptions.

He said to the Vali Zid: "'You have, without any cause, wrought my destruction. It is not the European you have injured, but me." But Zid bin Juma said: "No one but Mohammed bin Kasum, can have shot him. Just now in the night I heard shots. They must have come back then." Next morning Zid sent messengers out to call all the Arabs together and likewise informed the Sultan. Thereupon the same morning came messengers from Sike, who sent his servant Sungura and a message that he knew nothing about it. Yet he was in the same boat with Mohammed bin Kasum. Many Arabs also came, and Mohammed bin Kasum among them. Suddenly an Englishman also appeared who was at Urambo.

'A great examination was set on foot and the Arabs said: "We know nothing of the matter." Then up jumped Sleman bin Zahir el Gabiri, and said in the presence of Mohammed: "No one can have shot the European but Mohammed bin Kasum. He is a great robber!" Then Mohammed grew alarmed and said: "I stole the ivory-that is true, but

I did not fire at the European. Should I kill a man who travels with Hamed bin Mohammed? I would never do such a thing." Sleman said: "It was you and no one else. If you bid us, Hamed bin Mohammed, we will put him in chains and give him to you, that you may take him to the coast." I said to them: "You people of Tabora yourselves take him prisoner."

'Thereupon the Englishman who came from Urambo said to me: "Let us go and see to Mr. Giesecke." So we went and came to Ituru, where we found Dr. Junker. He said to us: "The missionaries have taken Giesecke with them." We lay down to sleep, and next morning I went with Junker and the Englishman to the missionaries, where we found Giesecke. He was sick and called me and said: "I am sick-God knows it. The ivory that I have has brought me to ruin; if you leave me in the lurch it will all be lost. I beg of you, take it and give it to my friends on the coast. Say what you want for doing so." I answered him: "I want nothing for it, but tell these Europeans-the Frenchmen, the Englishman, and Junker-to count the tusks, then I will take them with me." Then he said to me: "Leave me eight men here to look after me." Then I went back with the Europeans to Ituru, where they counted the ivory. When we had finished the counting the missionaries went home, and the Englishman asked me for guides to Tabora. Two days later we set out and reached the coast near Bagamoyo.'

Poor Giesecke received the tenderest care among the White Fathers, but nevertheless succumbed to his wounds on October 3. His murderer, Mohammed bin Kasam, thanks to the disturbed state of affairs, long evaded the arm of justice, but at last ventured to visit the coast, and was condemned to death by a court-martial on June 16, 1890. On the 25th of the same month he was hanged.

The rest of the ivory belonging to the firm of H. A. Meyer was conscientiously delivered by Tippu Tip at Zanzibar. Their other claims for compensation, which amounted to 80,000 marks in round numbers, were only partially satisfied, in spite of repeated representations to Seyyid Bargash and his successor, Khalifa. A *shamba* belonging to the murderer was confiscated for their benefit and sold for 1,900 dollars, also a quantity of ivory belonging to his accomplice, Zid bin Juma, which produced some 2,000 marks, was seized on the coast.

Dr. Junker reached Zanzibar under Tippu Tip's guidance. He proceeded to Europe and recorded the experiences and knowledge acquired on his long voyages in various articles which appeared in 'Petermann's Mitteilungen,' and a larger work, 'Reisen in Afrika, 1875-1886.' He died at St. Petersburg in 1892.

When Tippu Tip reached the coast at Bagamoyo, he found a letter from the Sultan summoning him to come to him at once. He immediately obeyed, and as soon as he reached Zanzibar was received by Seyyid Bargash. He had much to tell the Sultan about his last journey, and the latter learned with sorrow how from the West also the Europeans were pressing ever closer upon the old bulwarks of the Arabs on the mainland. The reports of so experienced a traveller convinced him that his part in the interior of Africa would before long be played out. In two voyages to Europe this clear-sighted Prince had learned from personal observation the power of the West, and had of late been forced to realize in his own country how weak his Oriental despotism was compared with the armaments of

Germany and England. He had no further aspiration than to retain at least the remainder of his kingdom-the island of Zanzibar itself-and he closed his interview with his subject, who had travelled so far and saw through matters with the same hopeless perspicacity, with these mournful words: 'Then he said to me: "Hamed, be not angry with me; I want to have no more to do with the mainland. The Europeans want to take Zanzibar here from me: how should I be able to keep the mainland? Happy are those who did not live to see the present state of affairs. You are a stranger here still, but you will see how things are going here."'

And Tippu Tip adds with resignation: 'When I heard these words I knew that it was all up with us.'

Native drawing water from the wells

Native men on a donkey

CHAPTER XIII

THE FIGHTING ROUND STANLEY FALLS

'Dulce et decorum est pro patriâ mori.'
HORACE.

Two months after his arrival at Zanzibar Tippu Tip learned that soon after his departure from Stanley Falls a violent conflict had broken out between the Arabs and Europeans, ending in the flight of the latter and the destruction of the station. The autobiographer says nothing as to the details of these events, and they might quite properly be left out here, as he himself was not present; but the way in which the hostile parties rush at each other and the long accumulated store of explosive material breaks into flame at a touch is so characteristic, the devotion even to death of the slender body of Europeans so admirable, that it may be worth while to insert here the narrative of an eye-witness, who seems qualified beyond all others to give an account of this deplorable episode.

Deane, then the head of the station, who, as the only surviving European, defended it to the last charge of powder, and only by a miracle escaped the fury of his Arab pursuers, shortly before his death gave Herbert Ward, a traveller whom we shall meet again in the career of our hero, a description of his sufferings, which the latter thus reproduces in his 'Five Years with the Congo Cannibals' (Part II., chap. xi.):

'You know how I was ordered to Stanley Falls last year (1885) by the Colonel (Sir Francis de Winton, the Administrator-General of the Congo State) to take over command and endeavour to keep the Arabs in order and protect the natives from their exactions, so that the authority of the State might be established and fully recognised by them. Well, you remember how I got wounded in the leg by a spear-thrust when the Monungeri savages attacked us on the first journey up to the Falls, and how I had to return to Stanley Pool to recover from the effects of the wound, for we found that the spear had been poisoned. I lay ill a long while, and it was only in January that I was able to return to the Falls.

'You remember-for I showed you my instructions-how I was promised a plentiful supply of ammunition and rifles and reinforcements of men when the river steamer *Le Stanley* made its next trip up to the Falls, Which would be in August. Well, upon my arrival I found things in a very bad condition: the Arabs had the entire upper hand and bullied the natives just as they pleased; yet I could do nothing to prevent them, for it was too far off the time of my expected reinforcements to provoke a conflict.

'Tippu Tip had gone back to Zanzibar, and had left his partner, Bwana Nzige, in charge of his people, and Nzige's son, Rashid bin Mohammed bin Said, also had much to say in the management of affairs during Tippu Tip's absence. I soon saw that these fellows did not like me or my ways at all, and that I should not get them to conform to my orders without a row. I had thirty-two Haussas, under Sergeant-Major Musa Kanu, a fine, tall fellow, and also about forty Bangala, whom I had brought up with me in *Le Stanley*, and I set to work to fortify the station, clear away the grass and scrub around it in case of a surprise, and to be able to keep an eye on the Arabs over on the mainland.

'It is necessary to observe that the State station of Stanley Falls was built on an island in the Congo just below the seventh cataract, while the Arabs were mostly on the mainland, although a few lived in a village on the same island among the natives.

'Well, the time went on, and a worse feeling sprang up between the Arabs and me, owing to my attempts to protect the natives from their robberies. One day, about the middle of July (1886), a woman entered the camp seeking protection and saying that the Arabs had flogged her. Her story was that she had been given to Tippu Tip as a pledge of friendship by her father, but that, being of the Wachongera Meno tribe (*i.e.*, of "the filed teeth" tribes, who are usually cannibals), Tippu Tip did not care for her, and had given her to one of his most influential Arab headmen. This Arab ill-treated her, she said, and so she had fled to us for protection. I could not discover any traces of ill-treatment-there were no marks on her skin- and I told her she must return to her Arab husband, as I had no right to interfere unless she were being cruelly used, and I had her conducted back to the Arab village. After a few days she came into the station again, with her back cut with lashes from a whip and her body covered with bruises, telling us that she had been terribly flogged, and that, had she not escaped, her master would have killed her. This time there was no doubt her story was true. She was a pitiable-looking object, and I determined nothing should induce me to give her up again to the cruelty and brutality of the Arabs. It was not long before Bwana Nzige, with his son Rashid and all the principal Arabs, came over to me and demanded the woman's release. I replied that I should not think of letting her be taken away again to suffer their brutal violence, and that I was sent to the country to prevent such acts, and that, as the representative of the Congo Free State, I intended to do my duty. As the woman represented a certain value to them, I was quite prepared to pay, on behalf of the Government, whatever they should demand in reason as ransom. They sullenly declined this offer and persistently demanded the release of the woman, saying that I should regret my refusal. Then I knew that the storm which had been so long brewing was going to break. However, we were well armed, my Haussas were plucky, and the fortifications I had constructed protected us well, and I considered that, with the aid of my two Krupp guns, we could keep the Arabs at a respectful distance, and in a few days-for it was the month of August-I hoped to see *Le Stanley* arrive with reinforcements and ammunition and a white officer or two, for I was alone, as you know.

'The Arabs made no direct attack upon us, although large numbers of their Manyemas continued to assemble on the mainland. At last *Le Stanley* was signalled early one morning coming up the river, and I was indeed delighted, for I expected she would have on board the much-needed ammunition and reinforcements. But imagine my disgust when, on getting to the landing-place, I found she had not brought me a single cartridge of the promised 10,000, not a rifle, and not a man, save only Lieutenant Dubois, of the

Belgian Lancers. He turned out to be a splendid fellow; but still I needed the other things, or my fight was hopeless.

'Well, when *Le Stanley* arrived the Arabs came to the conclusion that I should prove too strong for them with my supposed reinforcements, so they sent in a deputation to intimate that hostilities were at an end, and that they desired to remain in friendly relations with the white man who represented the Congo Free State. I agreed to this, and we parted, seemingly good friends, and shortly afterwards I even went so far as to visit one of their villages at the upper end of the island, and there found, to my chagrin, some of the Zanzibar crew of *Le Stanley* chatting with their compatriots among the Arabs, and telling them of my disappointment, and how the steamer had brought me none of the expected aid.

'The next day *Le Stanley* left, and Dubois was busy arranging his quarters while I glanced through the piles of newspapers that my considerate friends on the Lower Congo had sent up to me. Towards evening I was told by a friendly native that the Arabs intended attacking the station the following morning, for he had overheard their plans. We kept strict watch during the night, but could distinguish nothing, until at dawn we found sure enough a large body of Manyemas had crossed from the mainland in the night and entrenched themselves on my island, about 800 yards from the stockade. As soon as it was light we received a practical proof of their hostility, for they fired upon us. We kept up a lively fire upon them with our Snyder and Martini rifles for two days; but they were well sheltered by their rough earthworks, and there were no serious losses on either side.

'Our men kept up a tremendous fusillade whenever the Arabs made any signs of attacking, and on the evening of the third day Dubois sallied out of the stockade and penetrated into the Arab lines, capturing a Manyema drum, which they left in their flight. It was hot work, and he got his revolverpouch shot off his hip. That night they remained quiet, but in the morning fresh earth-heaps were found thrown up nearer our entrenchments, and the fight recommenced. Our ammunition was now beginning to fail, and so we could not waste so many shots, and the Arabs took advantage of this to make two or three rushes right up to our position; but we drove them back each time, and I worked the Krupp guns so hard that blood came from my ears, and I knocked the end off my little finger by getting it jammed in the breach. My boys-Jack (poor little Jack from Manyanga, down there in the valley), and the two Aruwimi youngsters-behaved splendidly, bringing ammunition to us, and making tea and carrying the cups up to us right across the Arab line of fire. Dubois charged out again, and drove them back, and then darkness set in and stopped the fight for the night. The Bangala deserted that night, taking some native canoes and making off down the river, to try and reach Bangala, which, you know, is a 500 miles' journey.

'In the morning the fight started again. We could now do little but work the Krupp guns, as the little rifle ammunition we had left was almost entirely bad.

'We got cap-guns and old trade flint-locks out of the store, and gave them to the Haussas to fire; but seven of these poor chaps were already dead, and the rest, save Musa Kanu and three men, came to me that evening and said they must go. It was no use fighting when they were bound to fall into the hands of the Arabs. I threatened to shoot them as deserters, and they replied:

"'Very well, master, you shoot us. We would rather you shoot us than have our throats cut by the Arabs."

'And as soon as darkness set in they made off to the canoes and drifted down river after the Bangala.

'Dubois and I were now left with only four Haussas and Samba, a native of the Aruwimi, who had been freed by the State, and worked faithfully with me during all my stay at the Falls; and despairingly we determined to destroy that night all that we could of the stores remaining, to spike the guns and blow up the station, and make off into the woods, to hide until relief should come from Bangala, where we reckoned the fugitive Bangalas would arrive by a certain date, and Coquilhat would hurry up in the steamer *Association Internationale Africaine* to our relief. We sprinkled the stores with oil, piled up the cartridges, spiked the Krupps, and gathered all the loose gunpowder together, and, having set a train to this outside the station, we two, with Musa Kanu and his three faithful Haussas and Samba, who refused to budge without us, made off under cover of the darkness to gain the north shore, and seek shelter in the woods there.

'I was the last to leave the place, and I set fire to the train of powder and made after the rest.

'The night was pitch dark, and the station was blazing brightly behind us, but somehow the powder had not exploded. We knew the Arabs must have discovered our flight by this time, so we hurried along to cross over to the mainland. We had to wade through an arm of the Congo-a rushing torrent of water, about 50 yards wide and generally at that season only waist-deep. Dubois slipped on the rocks, and was swept down into deeper water. I knew he could not swim, so I at once jumped in after him, and managed to catch hold of him before he was carried away by the swift current. We were just able to reach the steep rocky bank, and, exhausted, I told Dubois to hold on to the edge of a jutting rock, while the Haussas, having safely passed over, came to our assistance along the top of the bank. Musa Kanu undid his belt and gun-strap, tied them together, and lowered them to me; but when I turned where Dubois had been, saying, "Catch hold here!" I could see nothing of him. There was no Dubois.

'By the light of the burning station, where the cartridges and gunpowder had now commenced to explode, illuminating vividly for a moment the surrounding scene, I searched the water for any signs of Dubois; but alas, poor fellow! he had become numbed in the water, or his heavy boots pulled him down, and he had been swept away by the current. It was the last I ever saw of him, and my grief and misery were so great at the loss of my only friend away up here, after all the pluck he had shown during the four days' fighting at the station, that I wept, while the Haussas, after pulling me up, cried too.

'We were indeed a wretched lot. My clothes had been burnt off me and torn in the fight. I had only an old blanket round me and a shirt on, but no boots; and sadly, and feeling that I didn't care if the Arabs should find me and end the wretchedness at once, I crept away into the forest.'

There he remained for thirty days, often on the verge of starvation, and hunted by the Arabs from one hiding-place to another, till at last the steamer *Association Interna-*

tionale Africaine from Bangala brought him deliverance. After all, a long life was not in store for him. When he had restored his shattered health in England, he returned to the Congo State, and met his death in an elephant hunt in the forests of the Lukolela. His station remained for the time in the hands of the Arabs, till the events occurred which we shall describe in the next chapter.

Women in veil

CHAPTER XIV

THE EMIN PASHA EXPEDITION

'Nihil est quod noscere malim
Quam fluvii causas per sæcula tanta latentes,
Ignotumque caput, spes sit mihi certa videndi
Niliacos fontes.'

                            LUCAN: *Pharsalia.*

Mention has been made in a previous chapter of the Egyptian general Emin Pasha. Such is the name under which in the eighties of last century Edmund Schnitzer, a German savant, became known to the whole civilized world. He was born, in 1840, at Oppeln, of Jewish parents, afterwards became a convert to Christianity, and studied medicine and science at Breslau. In 1865 he became port physician at Antivari, in Albania, and from 1873 on made lengthy journeys in Armenia, Syria, and Arabia in the suite of a Turkish dignitary. In 1876 he entered the Egyptian service as Emin Effendi, and was there attached to the staff of Governor-General Gordon. With him he travelled about Khartoum and Uganda. In 1879 he was promoted to be Bey, and appointed Governor of the Equatorial Province. Here he found the chance of bringing his great administrative talents into play. His district, till then the scene of devastating slave-raids, soon recovered its prosperity under his rule. He established new stations, which made the country secure, and constructed an extensive network of roads. By the introduction of new cereals he forwarded agriculture, while cattlebreeding, which had been much neglected during years of fighting, soon attained its old importance, thanks to the peaceful progress of the country. In addition, Emin rendered great services to knowledge in the most various fields. As a geographer, he explored the still little known country round Lake Victoria. An exceptionally gifted linguist, he diligently studied the languages of the districts he passed through, and he benefited natural science by rich ornithological collections.

While he was thus engaged in the peaceful work of civilization in the heart of Africa, bloody conflicts were taking place in the North of Egypt. The growing influence of England and France on the government of the country had for years been awaking a feeling of hostility to foreigners. In June, 1882, a revolt broke out in Alexandria, instigated by the former War Minister, Arabi, in which many Europeans fell victims. The city was in consequence bombarded by the British Admiral Seymour on July 11 and 12; but the only result of this step was that the fury of the populace against the foreigners was augmented. True, the English managed, on September 13, to defeat Arabi at Tel-el-Kebir and take prisoner, and bring the Khedive, who had fled on the outbreak of the revolt, back to Cairo; but it was only a seeming peace which had been imposed. Already the national Islamic movement had found a new leader in Mohammed Ahmed, the Mahdi, who, under the pretext of a Divine mission, incited religious fanaticism and political discontent to take arms against the helpless central authority. Several brilliant victories which he gained over considerable armies commanded by English generals soon made him master of the whole of the Sudan, which intruded itself like a huge wedge between the seat of the Egyptian Government and Emin's district. After April 14, 1883, the latter found himself cut off from all communication with North Egypt.* Even in his own province the situation was beginning to be critical. The Mahdists, pressing further and further forward, tried to incite his subjects to join their movement, and in May, 1884, one of his higher officials, Ibrahim Aga, formally repudiated his authority. When, in addition, in 1885, a famine broke out in the north of his territory, between Lado and Dufilé, Emin found himself compelled to withdraw further to the southward. He went up the Nile to Wadelai, which he reached on July 10, and which became for the future the seat of his government.

Early in 1886 Emin received from Cairo the official announcement that the whole Sudan was abandoned. It was left to his own discretion to remain or go. Emin for some time entertained the idea of marching to the East Coast, but his troops refused to follow him. Besides, the plan would have been wrecked by the hostility of King Mwanga, of Uganda, who, as will be remembered, had about the same time refused a passage through his territories to Fischer, who was marching to Emin's relief.

While Emin thus clung to his post, cut off from all the world, a committee for his relief was forming under the presidency of Sir William Mackinnon, Bart. The subscriptions, to which the Egyptian Government contributed £10,000, quickly reached the total of £21,500. With this sum an expedition was to be sent to try and get through to the Pasha and release him from his dangerous position. The American Stanley, then at the zenith of his fame, was fixed on as the leader of the enterprise. After carefully weighing the possible routes, four in all, which came under consideration, he decided to advance from the mouth of the Congo to the Albert Nyanza, near which Emin must be located. By this river, which has the most abundant flow of water in Africa, one could go by steamer, with few slight interruptions, caused by the well-known cataracts, as far as the mouth of the Aruwimi, and then follow that stream up to Yambuya. After that there were about 400 miles to

---

*Since 1883 there had been in Emin's neighbourhood and under his protection two European travellers, who had escaped from the neighbouring countries, Dr. Junker, already mentioned, and Gaetano Casati, an Italian ex-officer, who since 1880 had been exploring for the Societá d'Esploracione Commerciale in Bahr el Ghazal and the Mombuttu countries. Both fugitives shared for three years the cares and perils to which Emin was exposed in his forlorn post, and repaid the hospitality shown them by much active support. Early in 1886 Junker, as we have seen, departed via Unyamwezi to the coast, while Casati proceeded in May of the same year to negotiate with King Kabarega, but was treated there more as a prisoner than as a guest, and in the end was actually condemned to death. On the approach of Stanley he was set at liberty, and in 1889 went on with him and Emin to the East Coast.

march, through districts which, it is true, were totally unknown, and probably covered with the densest forest; but Stanley had ere now overcome so many difficulties that such prospects could not daunt him. King Leopold not only gave a ready assent to the expedition traversing the Congo State, but placed at their disposal the Free State's entire supply of boats for the voyage up the Congo.

But there was a serious objection to this route-viz., the probable attitude of the Arabs. After the conflicts described in the last chapter, it was to be feared that they would treat any European passing through as an enemy. But Stanley had a brilliant idea for coping with this contingency too. He decided on nothing less than obtaining the co-operation in his enterprise of the leader of those very Arabs-our hero, Tippu Tip.

From Egypt, where he had been negotiating with the Government, Stanley proceeded, early in 1887, to Zanzibar. He arrived there in February, and found everything in good order for a start. The firm of Smith, Mackenzie and Co. had engaged carriers for him, provided the necessary goods, and got ready the steamer *Madura*, which was to carry the expedition round the Cape to the Congo. His first care at Zanzibar was to come to an understanding with Tippu Tip. The negotiations were carried on at the British Consulate-General. The entry of our hero seems to have been most dramatic. His adherents had sent him from Stanley Falls three Krupp shells, which he had had carried after him. Pointing to them, he said to Stanley that such were the presents he had to expect from Europeans. Stanley earnestly urged him to let bygones be bygones. Those conflicts had been brought about through the unfortunate misunderstandings of young people, and both sides had paid dearly for their hot-headedness. The King of the Belgians, at any rate, desired peace with the Arabs, and as a proof of it offered him, Tippu Tip, the post of Governor in the province wrested from the Congo State by the Arab bands.

The King had, in fact, given his consent by telegraph to this proposal, but the idea originated with Stanley, and does all honour to his political sagacity. There was no simpler way of check-mating his opponents than by making their leader his friend. And Stanley saw through his man clearly enough to be certain that his offer would not be rejected. Tippu Tip soon recovered his oriental repose in face of the propitiatory attitude of Stanley, and received his surprising proposal with his own peculiar blink, a sign with him of quick understanding. After the conditions had been conveyed to him in detail, he gave his consent. He was engaged at a monthly salary of £30, for which he was to pledge himself to hoist the Belgian flag and restrain his fellow-tribesmen from slave-hunting and other marauding. A European official was attached to him, who was to make regular reports to the King of the Belgians, and whose duty it was, besides, though nothing was said about this to Tippu Tip, to keep a watch on his supposed superior.

Such was the political side of the treaty, which had to be settled in order to afford a basis for the second, the commercial one, which was much more important to Stanley's present enterprise. Through all his scientific and political undertakings he had always remained a good man of business, and as such let it be known that Emin was presumably in possession of some 75 tons of ivory, which at a low computation represented a value of about £10,000. Tippu Tip was to provide the carriers necessary to convey this ivory to the coast, and thus cover most of the cost of the expedition. These were further to serve the purpose of conveying the ammunition intended for Emin's relief from the Congo to the Albert Nyanza.

The two high contracting parties, after long haggling, agreed that Tippu Tip should furnish 600 carriers, for whom he was to get £6 per head for the journey from Stanley Falls to the lake and back. Stanley, on his part, pledged himself to secure Tippu Tip and ninety-six followers free passage to the Congo, including provisions, and to conduct the caravan from there on to Stanley Falls.

After a farewell visit to the Sultan, productive of many presents to both travellers, the *Madura* put to sea on February 25, 1887. At Cape Town, where they put in, Tippu Tip had for the first time an opportunity of making acquaintance with a European town. The impression was, according to Stanley, so tremendous that he declared he was now beginning to admire Europeans. So far he had regarded them all as more or less fools, but now he realized that they were far superior to the Arabs. To Stanley's proposal that he should come with him some day to London, and there make acquaintance with the Europeans and their works at the fountain-head, he answered, like a good Moslem, with the pious words, 'In sha Allah' (if God wills), 'I shall go there.' And there it has been left until to-day. His means would have long since allowed of his making a voyage to 'Ulaya,'* but, notwithstanding all the offers made him, he has never got further than being ready to go. Allah has not yet willed it.

On March 18 the *Madura* reached the mouth of the Congo. The prospects of the voyage up the river were very unfavourable, as the steamers expected were not available. At length they succeeded in chartering some craft, which next day conveyed the expedition to Matadi, a spot 110 from the miles from the mouth. From there, owing to the rapids, they had to march on foot. In a discontented mood, due mainly to disputes between the various tribes composing the caravan, they proceeded on March 21 towards Leopoldville, which was reached on April 21. Here the difficulties as to procuring steamers were repeated, but at last they succeeded in shipping the whole expedition. But the vessels proved so defective that on May 12, at Bolobo, it became necessary to divide the caravan into two parts. The advance column, consisting of the healthiest men, under Stanley's personal leadership, was to sail up the Congo and Aruwimi as far as Yambuya, and from there, as speed was necessary, at once to take the land route eastwards to the Albert Nyanza. As soon as they were disembarked, the fastest of the steamers was to turn back and pick up the rear column at Bolobo. According to Stanley's reckoning, they also could reach Yambuya within six weeks, and there they were to take over the loads left behind, which were to be conveyed by the carriers Tippu Tip was to supply, and follow the advance column as quickly as possible.

This division of the expedition into two parts was the prelude to very tragic events, which ended in the almost total loss of the rear column.

Attached to it were five Englishmen: (1) Major Barttelot, 'a generous, frank, and chivalrous young officer, distinguished in Afghanistan and on the Sudanese Nile for pluck

---

* 'Ulaya,' from the Arabic 'Vilaje,' is the Swahili expression for Europe.

and performance of duty'*; (2) his friend, a young civilian named Jameson, a gentleman of wealth with a passion for natural history studies, whose alacrity, capacity, and willingness to work were reported to be 'unbounded'; (3) Herbert Ward, mentioned in the previous chapter, who had long worked in Borneo, New Zealand, and the Congo country, and was spoken of as bright, intelligent, and capable; (4) John Rose Troup, who had proved himself 'an industrious and zealous officer' under Stanley in the Congo State; and (5) William Bonny, who had seen service in the Zulu and Nile campaigns, and was reputed 'a staid and observing man.'

The first-named was in all respects marked out for the chief command, a post for which, in Stanley's judgment, he was thoroughly suited. Jameson was to be second to him, and to take his place in case he was incapacitated.

On June 16 Stanley arrived at Yambuya, Barttelot having parted with him on the way to escort Tippu Tip in a special steamer to his old station. The latter reports as follows:

'At last we came to the River Usoko, which higher up is called Mature. Stanley turned aside with all his boats towards the places where many of my men had been killed when they were marching with Salum bin Mohammed. His caravan now proceeded by that river with the steamboats. They gave the Major and me a boat to bring us to Stanley Falls. So we came to that place. And l had asked Stanley for powder, so that I might arm the 500 men whom I was to provide, if I could get them; but he said: "I cannot spare you any of the powder I have, but buy some there at Stanley Falls." I had also got Belgian flags, which I was to hoist everywhere in the districts which I ruled. I hoisted one at Stanley Falls when I arrived, and there on the Usoko my men hoisted the flag wherever they came. At Stanley Falls I ran it up on a mast. The Major departed, and we took leave of each other.'

On June 25 Barttelot reached Yambuya, and on the 28th Stanley began his rapid advance to the Albert Nyanza. Before leaving he delivered to the commander of the rearguard the following instructions:*

'*June* 24*th*, 1887.
'To Major Barttelot, etc.
'SIR,

'As the senior of those officers accompanying me on the Emin Pasha Relief Expedition, the command of this important post naturally devolves on you. It is also for the interest of the Expedition that you accept this command, from the fact that your Sudanese company, being only soldiers and more capable of garrison duty than the Zanzibaris, will be better utilized than on the road.

'The steamer *Stanley* left Yambuya on the 22nd of this month for Stanley Pool. If she meets with no mischance she ought to be at Leopoldville on the 2nd of July. In two days more she will be loaded with about 500 loads of our goods, which were left in charge

---

* *Cf.* 'In Darkest Africa,' vol. i., pp. 471-473.

* 'In Darkest Africa,' vol.i., p. 114.

of Mr. J. R. Troup. This gentleman will embark, and on the 4th of July I assume that the *Stanley* will commence her ascent of the river, and arrive at Bolobo on the 9th. Fuel being ready, the 125 men in charge of Messrs. Ward and Bonny, now at Bolobo, will embark, and the steamer will continue her journey. She will be at Bangala on the 19th of July, and arrive here on the 31st of July. Of course, the lowness of the river in that month may delay her a few days, but, having great confidence in her captain, you may certainly expect her before the 10th of August.

'It is the non-arrival of these goods and men which compel me to appoint you as commander of this post. But as I shall shortly expect the arrival of a strong reinforcement of men, greatly exceeding the advance force, which must, at all hazards, push on to the rescue of Emin Pasha, I hope you will not be detained longer than a few days after the departure of the *Stanley* on her final return to Stanley Pool in August.

'Meantime, pending the arrival of our men and goods, it behoves you to be very alert and wary in the command of this stockaded camp. Though the camp is favourably situated and naturally strong, a brave enemy would find it no difficult task to capture if the commander is lax in discipline, vigour, and energy. Therefore I feel sure that I have made a wise choice in selecting you to guard our interests here during our absence.

'The interests now entrusted to you are of vital importance to this Expedition. The men you will eventually have under you consist of more than an entire third of the Expedition. The goods that will be brought up are the currency needed for transit through the regions beyond the lakes; there will be a vast store of ammunition and provisions, which are of equal importance to us. The loss of these men and goods would be certain ruin to us, and the advance force itself would need to solicit relief in its turn. Therefore, weighing this matter well, I hope you will spare no pains to maintain order and discipline in your camp, and make your defences complete and keep them in such a condition that, however brave an enemy may be, he can make no impression on them. For this latter purpose I would recommend you to make an artificial ditch 6 feet wide, 3 feet deep, leading from the natural ditch, where the spring is round the stockade. A platform, like that on the southern side of the camp, constructed near the eastern as well as the western gate, would be of advantage to the strength of the camp. For remember, it is not the natives alone who may wish to assail you, but the Arabs and their followers may, through some cause or other, quarrel with you and assail your camp.

'Our course from here will be due east, or by magnetic compass east by south as near as possible. Certain marches that we may make may not exactly lead in the direction aimed at. Nevertheless, it is the south-west corner of Lake Albert, near or at Kavalli, that is our destination. When we arrive there we shall form a strong camp in the neighbourhood, launch our boat, and steer for Kibero, in Unyoro, to hear from Signor Casati, if he is there, of the condition of Emin Pasha. If the latter is alive, and in the neighbourhood of the lake, we shall communicate with him, and our after conduct must be guided by what we shall learn of the intentions of Emin Pasha. We may assume that we shall not be longer than a fortnight with him before deciding on our return towards the camp along the same road traversed by us.

'We will endeavour, by blazing trees and cutting saplings along our road, to leave sufficient traces of the route taken by us. We shall always take, by preference, tracks leading east-ward. At all crossings where paths intersect we shall hoe up and make a hole a few inches deep across all paths not used by us, besides blazing trees when possible.

'It may happen, should Tippu-Tip have sent the full number of adults promised by him to me, viz., 600 men (able to carry loads), and the *Stanley* has arrived safely with the 125 men left by me at Bolobo, that you will feel yourself sufficiently competent to march the column, with all the goods brought by the *Stanley* and those left by me at Yambuya, along the road pursued by me. In that event, which would be very desirable, you will follow closely our route, and before many days we should most assuredly meet. No doubt you will find our *bomas* intact and standing, and you should endeavour to make your marches so that you could utilize these as you marched. Better guides than those *bomas* of our route could not be made. If you do not meet them in the course of two day's march you may rest assured that you are not on our route.

'It may happen, also, that though Tippu-Tip has sent some men, he has not sent enough to carry the goods with your own force. In that case you will, of course, use your discretion as to what goods you can dispense with to enable you to march. For this purpose you should study your list attentively.

'1. Ammunition, especially fixed, is most important.
'2. Beads, brass wire, cowries and fabric, rank next.
'3. Private luggage.
'4. Powder and caps.
'5. European provisions.
'6. Brass rods as used on the Congo.
'7. Provisions (rice, beans, peas, millet, biscuits).

'Therefore you must consider, after rope, sacking, tools, such as shovels (never discard an axe or bill-hook), how many sacks of provisions you can distribute among your men to enable you to march-whether half your brass rods in the boxes could not go also and there stop. If you still cannot march, then it would be better to make two marches of six miles twice over if you prefer marching to staying for our arrival, than throw too many things away.

'With the *Stanley's* final departure from Yambuya you should not fail to send a report to Mr. William Mackinnon, c/o Gray, Dawes and Co., 13, Austin Friars, London, of what has happened at your camp in my absence, or when I started away eastward; whether you have heard of or from me at all, when you do expect to hear, and what you purpose doing. You should also send him a true copy of this order, that the Relief Committee may judge for themselves whether you have acted, or purpose to act, judiciously.

'Your present garrison shall consist of 80 rifles and from 40 to 50 supernumeraries. The *Stanley* is to bring you within a few weeks 50 more rifles and 75 supernumeraries, under Messrs. Troup, Ward, and Bonny.

'I associate Mr. J. S. Jameson with you at present. Messrs. Troup Ward, and Bonny will submit to your authority. In the ordinary duties of the defence and the conduct of the camp or of the march there is only one chief, which is yourself; but, should any vital step be proposed to be taken, I beg you will take the voice of Mr. Jameson also. And when Messrs. Troup and Ward are here, pray admit them to your confidence, and let them speak freely their opinions.

'I think I have written very clearly upon everything that strikes me as necessary. Your treatment of the natives, I suggest, should depend entirely upon their conduct to you. Suffer them to return to the neighbouring villages in peace, and if you can in any manner by moderation, small gifts occasionally of brass rods, etc., hasten an amicable intercourse, I should recommend you doing so. Lose no opportunity of obtaining all kinds of information respecting the natives, the position of the various villages in your neighbourhood, etc.

'I have the honour to be,
'Your obedient servant,
'HENRY M. STANLEY,
'Commanding Expedition.'

The pith and marrow of the directions was that, whatever happened, the rear column was to follow the advance as quickly as possible. Stanley had thought it quite within the range of possibility that Tippu Tip would either fail to furnish the promised carriers or else not supply enough, and he had fully discussed Tippu Tip's reliability with Barttelot after giving the latter his instructions. If this discussion took place as Stanley describes, it was clearly pointed out in the course of it that absolute reliance could not be placed on the Arab. The attempt to make a friend of him was a counsel of necessity, for without his goodwill, after the conflicts that had preceded between the Arabs and Belgians, a march through the districts to be traversed was impossible. But it was *a priori* doubtful whether, when brought within range of the influence of his revengeful fellow-tribesmen, he would carry out all the obligations he had undertaken, and still more uncertain after the disputes that had taken place between the European members of the caravan and Tippu Tip's followers, particularly his puffed-up nephew, Salum bin Mohammed.

Beside this, Tippu Tip had made Barttelot almost impossible promises at parting. He had said that he would despatch the 600 men he had engaged to supply within nine days. Stanley, who knew what the promises of Orientals were, saw at once that he would not do so. The Moslem, when speaking of anything he is going to do in the future, always adds, 'In sha Allah.' If he does not do it, it is just because God has not willed it. When Barttelot, in answer to Stanley's warnings, asked in perplexity why on earth they had had anything to do with the untrustworthy old campaigner, the wily American compared his Arab friend to the Maxim gun he had with him, which, so long as it worked properly, could do very good service, and was then of inestimable value. But it might happen to break down, owing to defective construction, wrong handling, or being tampered with by the enemy. In that case one had to trust to the rifles, which one also carried. Just so Tippu Tip, if he did not fail through his own falseness, unskilful handling, or hostile influence, would be most helpful to the column. But, if he should be faithless, other resources must be forthcoming; and these in this case were his own men, who were with the rearguard, or whom, if necessary, they would enlist on their own account.

Stanley's forebodings were only too terribly realized. Tippu Tip did indeed soon send off 500 men, but they only got as far as the mouth of the Aruwimi. That is just the spot where some years before Salum bin Mohammed's caravan had been massacred. This led their leader, Ali bin Mohammed, at once to start on a mock punitive expedition. He blazed away all his powder, did not dare go any further, and went back to Stanley Falls. This first attempt to obtain carriers was followed by various others. The officers of the rear column were constantly travelling to and fro between Yambuya, Stanley Falls, and Kassongo in search of Tippu Tip, whose own concerns took him now here, now there, to hold him to the fulfilment of his agreement.

It must not be assumed that he had maliciously neglected his engagements, as Stanley tries to make out. He had already shown his good intentions by getting ready in a remarkably short time 500 carriers, for whose non-arrival he was not directly to blame. Even if gross neglect could be brought home to him, there is much to be said in his defence. The supplying of carriers had not been made a primary stipulation of his engagement. He was first and foremost Governor of the Stanley Falls district, and, as such, had manifold duties, which called him this way and that. To-day he had to administer justice at Kassongo, to-morrow to suppress disorders on the Lomami. In addition to this, he was a merchant, and his mercantile concerns naturally were more to him than the success of Stanley, towards whom he felt himself exonerated after having once supplied 500 men. And he had obviously no inducement whatever to do anything extra for Stanley when his own experiences as to Stanley's promises are recollected.

The moral responsibility for the tragic fate of the rear column cannot in any way be imputed to Tippu Tip. First and foremost it falls on Stanley himself, who left behind a large number of his comrades under conditions the difficulties of which he knew and with which they showed themselves unable to cope. Next, the Europeans in charge of the rear column must be pronounced to have shown themselves quite incompetent, in face of those difficulties, when they arose. In the instructions given by Stanley the event of the carriers not being supplied had been expressly provided for. Should it so happen, the rear column was to endeavour, as best it could, to get on without outside assistance, and to follow by quite short marches. This was plainly laid down. Instead of this Barttelot let a whole year pass, during which the greater part of his men, who at a pinch could have made the journey alone, perished miserably.

At last he had collected a number of carriers which seemed to him sufficient, and decided on a start on June 14, 1888. In forty-three days' march the caravan covered ninety miles, to the village of Banalya, a station of Tippu Tip's, in charge of an Arab named Abdallah Karoni. With him the Major quarrelled, and so decided to journey back once more to Stanley Falls, which he had visited seven times in the course of the year, and complain to Tippu Tip. But he never lived to do so. On the morning of July 19 he was treacherously shot by a Manyema named Senga, whose wife he had told to stop making a noise. For a moment it seemed as if this was to be the signal for a general mutiny, but Bonny, the only Englishman still with the caravan, succeeded in mastering the excitement, though he could not prevent several loads being plundered.

Three days later Jameson came up with the last of the stragglers. According to the instructions, he was now to take over the command. In order to make himself quite secure for the future, he determined to induce Tippu Tip himself, by the offer of a large sum of money, to lead the caravan on to the Albert Nyanza, and for that purpose he went again to Stanley Falls. His arrival there and his negotiations with Tippu Tip are described as follows in the autobiography:

'After a month Jameson appeared and announced that the Major had been shot. His murderer was Senga, who, however, had escaped. Some other men too had fled, and about ten loads were missing. "But," he went on, "all the rest of the loads we have got together under guard at a place where there are townships near at hand, and all the rest of the people are there. And now I have come to ask you to accompany me." That meant myself and the Belgians. We asked him: "Why did Senga shoot the Major?" He replied: "Because he forbade him to get up a *ngoma*. And his *wanyampara** said: 'This *ngoma* is for joy at our starting. Is it right for us to be mournful, as at a funeral?' Then one evening between eight and nine the wives of Senga were singing, when the Major suddenly came and made passes with a spear at one of them. When her husband saw that, he fired at him. That is the reason." After four days they brought Senga and his wives and children in irons. I handed them over to the Belgians, and they asked him: "Why did you shoot the Major?" He replied in the same way as Jameson had told us. They said: "If anyone set you on, say so, for you will be executed anyhow." But he replied: "No one set me on; nor was there any other reason than what I have told you." Then the Belgians called me and Jameson, told us what Senga had said, and gave him up to Jameson. The latter ordered his execution. "But his belongings," he said, "are not implicated or to blame." So our slave Senga was shot.

'Jameson begged me to accompany him, but the Belgians said: "Hamid bin Mohammed must not go away. He is here in the service of the State, and we are under him, so how can he go away? It is in his agreement that he should give you men, but not that he is to go with you himself." Then Jameson promised to pay 50,000 to 60,000 dollars, offering to pay it out of his own money if they would not give it in Europe. But the Belgians answered him: "If you want Hamed bin Mohammed, go to Banana and telegraph. If he gets leave to conduct you, you can afterwards agree on his salary."'

Thereupon Jameson decided to ask at Brussels by telegraph, and proceeded down the river to hand in the despatch himself. But he only got as far as the Lomami, where he fell ill of fever and died. Of the remaining Europeans belonging to the expedition, Troup had been sent back to Europe very ill, while Ward had apparently had differences of opinion with the Major, and while waiting for the telegraphic instructions of the home Committee kept far away from the caravan on the Lower Congo.

The native portion of the rear column, now under Bonny's command, had also shrunk to half its numbers through illness and privation. In this woeful plight did Stanley

---

*Overseers of the caravan.

find his reserve, on which he had built such great hopes, when he returned from the Albert Nyanza to Banalya on August 17, 1888. After a most arduous march he had safely joined the Pasha, on April 29, at Kawalli, on the west shore of Albert Nyanza, and, after convincing himself that no danger threatened him for the moment, returned on June I to pick up the remainder of the expedition, left behind a year before on the Aruwimi.

Being now sufficiently provided with carriers, he returned on January 18, 1889, to the Albert Nyanza, and conducted the Pasha, who was very reluctant to abandon his post, half against his will, to the East Coast, which he reached-at Bagamoyo-on December 4. It is well known how Emin, who for more than ten years had braved the dangers of Central Africa, almost lost his life there by an accident. At a banquet given in his honour, the day after his arrival, by the German officials, owing to his shortsightedness, he fell out of the window, and sustained a fracture of the skull, which kept him for a long time on a sick bed. On recovering, he entered the service of the new German colony as Imperial Commissioner.

Zanzibar Stone Town

CHAPTER XV

RETURN TO ZANZIBAR-COLLAPSE OF THE ARAB POWER ON THE EAST COAST

'The old falls down, and time gives way to change,
And a new life arises from the ruins.'
SCHILLER: *Tell.*

When Stanley returned to Banalya in August, 1888, he at once wrote to Tippu Tip, inviting him to a conference. He, however, could not get away himself, and sent in his stead his nephew, Salum bin Mohammed to confer with the explorer. Stanley devotes several pages of his work to their interview, but what he wanted of Tippu Tip is not very clear. On the one hand, he demanded that the Arab chief should pay him back the passage of himself and his men from Zanzibar to Stanley Falls, and replace all goods that had been lost, threatening, if necessary, to enforce his claims with the help of the Sultan and the British Consul-General; on the other, a fresh contract seems to be again floating before his eyes, which he evidently expects to obtain cheaply by putting these demands forward.

Tippu Tip, however, refused to be intimidated by any threats, and remained in conscious innocence at his station, which of late had advanced mightily as a centre of trade. 'Every month came Europeans to the camp in two or three boats, and they all took ivory on board-often they had to leave some behind. Stanley Falls was quite full of Europeans, and all that you could wish for was to be had there. It was a great port, and everything that one desired was to be had. Belgian and French trading companies also came there, and everywhere flourishing towns arose. And every boat that came took on board ivory.

'And it was at Stanley Falls as on the coast. No one sent for anything from Zanzibar, or Tabora, or Ujiji; everything was to be procured on the spot.'

With the Europeans, especially the Belgians, Tippu Tip lived on the best of terms. Once the Governor himself visited him to discuss the fixing of an ivory tax. Our chronicler declares that the Congo State demanded a payment in kind of 5 pounds on every *frasila* (somewhat more than 14 per cent.). Tippu Tip agreed to this for his own ivory, but requested that only 3 pounds (about 9 per cent.) should be levied from the other Arabs. The request was granted, and the Arabs agreed to the arrangement.

I have found no mention elsewhere of any such arrangement for taxing Tippu Tip higher than other Arabs; but, as a fact, about the time he was Vali at Stanley Falls a tax in kind of 4 pounds was imposed. It is not impossible that, to make his fellow-tribesmen better disposed to the tax, he allowed himself to be treated less favourably, and procured them some mitigation. He eventually found ways and means to make his account out of it.

While he was thus attending to his duties in the service of a European Power, he received from home the news that his old patron, Seyyid Bargash, was dead. He had long been suffering, and ended his eventful life on March 27, 1888. The physical troubles which made his last years a burden were, however, trifling compared with the spiritual sufferings which darkened the evening of his life.

Bargash, as is well known, in 1870 ascended the throne of his father, left vacant by the eagerly expected death of his brother Majid. Like the former, the type of an aristocratic Arab and an Oriental despot from head to foot, he once more revived for his country the days of ancient splendour, which seemed to have been buried on the death of Said. The forays of his subjects into the dark interior, which he followed with interest and supported to the best of his power, brought rich treasures into the country, of which he took his share by levying considerable taxes. On the island itself agriculture, especially the cultivation of the clove, was in its fullest prosperity, and the Sultan did not content himself with the produce of his own plantations, but also laid a heavy tax on the crops of his subjects; 30 per cent. of all cloves had to be given over to him. He was also a keen man of business, and had a whole fleet of merchant ships afloat on the Indian Ocean.

The ample means thus obtained enabled him to display the pomp worthy of an Eastern Prince. The palace which he built for himself, and which still serves as a residence for his successor, is known, on account of its extravagant furnishing, as *Bet el Ajaib*, or the 'House of Wonders.' Numerous country houses, situated in the most beautiful parts of the island and still favourite resorts, are also his work. He not only shone in outward splendour, but, like a wise ruler, applied the treasures that came flowing to him to further the welfare of his subjects. He raised himself a lasting memorial by the construction of a magnificent aqueduct. From Khemkhen, an abundant spring to the north of the town, he brought down excellent drinking-water through miles of pipes, which may be drawn to this day by every inhabitant of Zanzibar, free of cost, from numberless fountains.

The days of power and splendour soon went by. The Europeans, who till now had stayed in the country as peaceful traders or journeyed into the interior as harmless explorers, began to become politically dangerous, and hence the events which we have already touched on in Chapter XII. Toward the close of his life Bargash had lost his possessions on the mainland, and the time was not far distant when the land of his fathers would fall wholly under Western control.

The news of Bargash's death was received by Tippu Tip via Europe, to which it had been telegraphed-another sign how the times had changed. Two decades before he, like so many of his compatriots, had set out from the East Coast, not knowing how the road would end, and, cut off for years from communication with home, had pressed further and further towards the west. Now the Westerners had advanced from the same quarter into the wilderness, whose depths he had penetrated, and there, with the superior discoveries of their genius, had secured the sovereignty for themselves. Their steamers plied on the African river which had been awaked from its sleep of thousands of years, and brought the furthest strongholds of the Arab slave-hunters into communication with European civilization.

Tippu Tip, who was always in favour of good relations with his rulers, at once sent to Bargash's successor, his brother Khalifa, an embassy to convey congratulations to him on his accession to the throne, and assure him of the allegiance of his influential subject. Tippu Tip's son Sef had shortly before set out for the coast, and could still be overtaken by couriers and instructed to appear as his father's spokesman before the new Sultan.

But our hero himself was soon warned in an unpleasant manner to return to Zanzibar. The King of the Belgians informed him that Stanley had made serious accusations against him. He was said to be guilty of the death of Major Barttelot, and by the breach of the duties he had undertaken by agreement with Stanley to have caused material damage to the expedition led by the latter; Stanley had cited him before the English court at Zanzibar; a great lawsuit was in prospect, and his property there had already been sequestrated. A legal summons would probably reach him shortly.

This news startled Tippu Tip out of his calm, and he at once determined to travel to Zanzibar to defend himself against the accusations raised against him. In March, 1890, he started, after having taken a most friendly leave of the Europeans at his station. Rashid, the son of his cousin and companion in arms Bwana Nzige, was made Vali in his place, while two Arab friends were to look after his commercial, interests during his absence.

His fellow-tribesmen at Stanley Falls endeavoured in every possible way to hold back Tippu Tip from making the journey to the coast; they feared that it might go badly with him before the judgment-seat of the Europeans. In the old familiar places, too, which he passed through-Nyangwe and Kasongo-the worst was prophesied, and he was advised rather to let all his property in Zanzibar go, and to enjoy his life here among his friends, far beyond the reach of the arm of the law. He had quite sufficient fortune left in the interior to live comfortably.

But Tippu Tip, in his superior wisdom, flung all these well-meant warnings to the winds. To begin with, he felt himself innocent, and thought he would be able to prove it on the coast. Secondly, he said to himself that, if the decision should really go against him, as things then stood he would not be safe from the vengeance of the Europeans, even in the farthest depths of the interior. Whom should he call to his aid against the firearms of the white men? What sort of warriors the Manyema were he had learnt years before, when with a handful of riflemen he conquered the tribes one after another, divided as they were by internal dissensions. He had meanwhile seen with his own eyes the superior power of the Europeans, and knew that nothing could be done against them with such undisciplined natives as he had at command.

He seems to have been very outspoken with the Arabs who were besetting him, and flung about him such expressions as 'nonsense' and 'silly fools.'

When even his friend Bwana Nzige urged him to resist the Europeans, his patience gave way altogether, and he rejoined quite tragically: 'Do you, too, speak in this manner? I always took you for a sensible man, and now you talk like that!'

On his way to Lake Tanganyika, Tippu Tip met Msabbah bin Njem, the Vali of that district, by whom he was told that Rumalisa, whose headquarters were at Ujiji, was arming to attack the Europeans west of the lake. Captain Jacques had started on an expedition there for the Belgian Anti-slavery Society, and all Arab slave-traders felt their most particular interests threatened by his appearance. It was easy for Rumalisa, with the hatred towards Europeans which, even apart from this provocation, was seething in them, to find numerous adherents for his hostile plans.

Tippu Tip had heard before this of the intentions of his vassal, and had energetically enjoined on him to refrain from all hostilities. In Mtoa he met him, and learned to his delight that nothing had come of the purposed attack. Rumalisa had indeed, in defiance of the commands of Tippu Tip, made all preparations for fighting; but the boat that was to bring the necessary powder across Lake Tanganyika luckily let in the water, and so he was forced to abstain from a struggle which would have damaged the interests of the Arabs at least as much as those of the Belgians. Later on, when Tippu Tip was out of the country, Rumalisa renewed the abortive attack, and by so doing initiated a period of severe conflicts, in which much blood was shed, and in the end the power of his fellow-tribesmen was totally broken.

Tippu Tip, who still considered himself in the service of the King of the Belgians, in accordance with the instructions he had received hoisted the blue flag with the golden star, then crossed Lake Tanganyika, and marched from Ujiji towards the home of his fathers, Tabora.

On the way he received letters from Zanzibar, among them the summons from the court already announced. Stanley had brought an action for 90,000 dollars (about £11,000) damages, and the English judge, Cracknall, informed him that unless he put in an appearance before the court within six months, judgment would be given against him.

A curious item in this summons was the fact that the Arabic text gave as plaintiffs 'Emin Pasha and his people,' of course meaning the Relief Committee. In any case the wording was calculated to bring about misunderstandings, and the Pasha, as soon as he learned the misuse of his name, issued a public declaration stating that he had nothing whatever to do with the suit; that, on the contrary, he had parted with Tippu Tip's people, who had escorted him to the coast, on the best of terms. This declaration was sent in print to all Arabs of consequence in Zanzibar, and a document of similar tenour was sent to Tippu Tip as well.

Emin Pasha was known to all those who had become intimate with him as particularly touchy, and had often shown plainly that he was capable of being seriously aggrieved over the merest trifles. In this case, however, more was at issue. He had just entered the service of the German Empire, and was on the point of beginning a long journey to the interior. When it was made to appear through the summons, read with interest by all Arabs, that he was at grievous feud with Tippu Tip, the uncrowned ruler of Central Africa, he had reason to expect the greatest hindrances on his journey, and so it is not to be wondered at that he did all he could to set right erroneous surmises which might attach to the wording of that summons.

That the English judge purposely designated the plaintiffs so ambiguously can scarcely be conceived, although to the end of his life he was a deadly hater of Germans and was no well-wisher of Emin. At all events, when his attention was drawn to the doubtfulness of the wording, he did nothing to dispel any doubts that might attach to it.

At Unyanyembe Tippu Tip could feel himself once more at home. His old friend Mirambo had indeed been dead some years, and his brother, who succeeded him, Mpanda Sharo, had also died meanwhile. The present ruler was a son of Mirambo's, who kept up the old friendship of his father for Tippu Tip, and received him respectfully, as his father would have done. At the English mission-house near Tabora a hospitable reception was also accorded him.

The changes which our hero this time found on his return in his native district were far greater than those which met his eyes on his previous visit. In order to depict them we must connect them with the events at which we broke off in Chapter XII-the historical description of the German acquisitions in East Africa.

In April, 1888, Seyyid Khalifa signed the treaty by which the coast of our present colony was leased out to the German East African Company. Besides the control of the Customs, all the sovereign rights hitherto exercised by the Sultan, especially that of justice, were transferred to the Company, which, as an external mark of its power, hoisted its own flag at all the places it occupied beside the red banner of the Sultan. In spite of the artistic design of the flag, which, in addition to the German colours, bears the Southern Cross as a crest-this outward act of 'taking seisin' was not at once followed by the actual subjugation of the territory ceded.

The native population from the first viewed their new masters with distrust. What was said before about the behaviour of the Tabora Arabs to the German merchants was here, in an increased degree, true of the whole population of the coast as regards the officials of the Company. To the jealousy of competition was added the fear of before long falling wholly under the sway of the Europeans, who, according to their view, would put a stop to much that hitherto had been a matter of course: in the first place, the slave-trade, by which, directly or indirectly, almost the whole population lived-the Arabs and Swahilis by going out on raids and making profit out of the sale of the slaves carried off, the Indians by supplying at a high price the powder necessary for these expeditions and advancing the other goods needed for such enterprises at a high rate of interest.

The discontent which was fermenting in all was easily stirred up by those elements, which had most to lose if greater order became generally prevalent. Among these were, above all, the many officials of the Sultan who had hitherto drawn a comfortable extra income from bribes and cheating the Customs, and saw themselves suddenly robbed of it. Then there were the local chiefs who had unconditionally recognised the overlordship of the Sultan, and now felt themselves threatened by the foreigners settled on the coast; these, too, were easily induced to join the movement against the interlopers. A convenient incitement in the universal indignation was religion, indifferent as the East African generally is to his soul's welfare. It was also alleged that the officers of the Company did not always show tact in dealing with the natives. They were mostly young and placed among unfamiliar conditions, so that blunders were likely to occur. Yet it may be confidently asserted that even the wisest and most temperate conduct would not have checked the movement.

The Sultan, who had only agreed to the coast treaty under compulsion, did nothing to quiet the disturbed spirits; on the contrary, he undoubtedly regarded the incipient hostilities with complacency, and as far as lay in his power supported the resistance* of the people of the coast to the new element.

The first open resistance was offered in August, 1888, at Pangani, where the Sultan's Vali tried to prevent the hoisting of the Company's flag. The appearance of two men-of-war, the *Möwe* and the *Carola*, restored tranquillity for the time being; but hardly were they gone when the two officers of the Company were made prisoners in their own house by the natives, and were only saved with difficulty by the intervention of the Englishman Mathews, the Sultan's well-known general and subsequently Prime Minister of Zanzibar. At Tanga and Bagamoyo also hostilities broke out in September. The soul of the rising was the Arab Bushir bin Salum el Harthi, who had won warlike fame in successful struggles with Mirambo, and even by armed resistance to Sultan Bargash. He also stirred up Bwana Heri, the influential Sultan of Useguha, the hinterland of Saadani, to resistance. The Company was quite powerless in face of the gathering rising; the German men-of-war could, of course, only intervene at the larger ports and were unable to enforce a lasting peace. Except Bagamoyo and Dar es Salaam, the whole north coast had to be given up, and at the end of the year the south also fell to the rebels. At Lindi and Mikindani the officers of the Company, when all resistance seemed hopeless, were just barely able to save themselves, while at Kilwa two brave officials paid for their heroic defence of the post entrusted to them with their lives.

Meanwhile, people at home had recognized that if they did not mean wholly to give up the German cause in the new regions, the Empire must adopt energetic measures. After brief negotiations with England and Portugal, our neighbours in East Africa, it was decided to blockade the entire coast between 10° 28' and 2° 10' of south latitude, so as to prevent the importation of munitions of war. This blockade was opened on December 2 by the German and English admirals Deinhardt and Fremantle. A further decisive step was taken when, on January 30, 1889, the Reichstag adopted a Bill* by which a sum of 2,000,000 marks was placed at the disposal of the State for the effectual protection of German interests in East Africa, and it was decided to entrust the carrying out of the necessary measures to an Imperial Commissioner.

To this post, as we know, Captain Hermann Wissmann was nominated. He had first made his reputation as an explorer by crossing the Dark Continent from west to east, as was mentioned in Chapter X, and during the years 1883-1885 had made successful journeys of exploration in the Congo Basin, while an expedition at the end of that year to the south of the newly-founded Congo State, forced on him against his will by the attitude of the Arabs, who were then at war with the Belgians, had been prolonged into a second crossing of Africa. After having thus, with short intervals, spent almost eight years of activity in the interior, he returned home in the summer of 1888. He had then been selected, together with Dr. Peters, to lead the expedition planned by the Germans for the relief of

---

*Cf. for what follows Rochus Schmidt, 'Geschichte des Araberaufstandes in Ostafrika.'

*In order to secure a majority in the Reichstag, the question of slavery was skilfully tacked to it. This secured the votes of the Centre. The same tactics had been previously adopted by Bismarck to force England to join in the blockade.

Emin Pasha, but at the last moment it was still possible to secure him for the post of Commissioner.

The preparations for the suppression of the rising were made with the utmost speed. At Wissmann's suggestion, native African tribes were employed, under the command of German officers and non-commissioned officers. With the assent of the Egyptian Government, 700 Sudanese were enlisted, and, after negotiations with Portugal, 100 Zulus. The Europeans appointed were twenty-one officers (including surgeons and officials) and forty non-commissioned officers.

On March 21, 1889, Wissmann reached Zanzibar, and from there, after a short stay with the leader of the German squadron, Admiral Deinhardt, proceeded to the mainland. On April 28, after an agreement concluded with the principal representative of the German East African Company, M. de St. Paul Illaire, the entire control of the Company's territory, exclusive of the Customs, was handed over to the Imperial Commissioner. On April 29 the first transport, with the Sudanese, reached Bagamoyo. On May 6 all the fighting force was assembled, and then followed in rapid succession the warlike incidents by which the resistance of the rebels was gradually broken.

On May 8 Bushiri's fortified camp near Bagamoyo was stormed, though he himself unfortunately escaped. Bwana Heri's headquarters at Saadani, which had been previously bombarded by the naval force without definite result, fell on June 6. Pangani fell on July 9, and about the same time Tanga was taken by the sailors. Meanwhile various attempts had been made to enter into peaceful negotiations with the rebels, but they led to no result. Sleman bin Nasor el Lemki, later well known in Europe as the Vali of Dar es Salaam, had been sent by the Commissioner to Pangani to treat with the Arabs there, but was received with musket shots and could not land. Tippu Tip's son Sef also tried in vain to make himself useful. Coming from the interior, he had reached the coast near Saadani with a great caravan of ivory, and with Wissmann's permission had taken on his treasures to Zanzibar. At Wissmann's request, he returned to Saadani to induce Bwana Heri to accept peace, but was not successful.

When Bushiri saw his power broken on the coast he withdrew further into the interior and attacked the town of Mpapwa, where the German East African Company had a settlement. This he destroyed. Wissmann followed him with a large force, reached Mpapwa on October 10, and established there a fresh and strongly fortified station.

Bushiri meanwhile had made off again. He had found numerous adherents among the warlike Wahehe and Mafiti, and hastened now to make use of the Commissioner's absence for a fresh advance on the coast. He had already penetrated as far as Usaramo, and his hordes had there practised the most inhuman cruelties, when Wissmann's lieutenant, Freiherr von Gravenreuth, advanced against him from Dar es Salaam. Near the township of Yombo he inflicted a serious defeat on the insurgents, but Bushiri again escaped. His auxiliaries, however, deserted him, and at length, after he had once more barely escaped with his life in an attack on the village of Masiro, Jumben Magaya succeeded in taking him prisoner at Kwa Mkoro, on the borders of Nguru. The chief, Dr. Schmidt, took him to Pangani, where he was hanged on December 15.

It now became necessary to break down the resistance of the powerful Bwana Heri, who was arming afresh in the hinterland of Saadani. A detachment sent out to reconnoitre under Rochus Schmidt on December 27 came unexpectedly at Mlembula on a strongly fortified *boma* in the bush, whose existence had hitherto been unknown. An attack on it was repulsed, whereupon Wissmann assembled all the fighting forces at his disposal for a fresh advance, and January 3, 1890, after a furious conflict, stormed the stronghold, which proved itself a model of African fortification.

Bwana Heri escaped, and assembled his troops at Palamakaa, a village five hours' march from Saadani, for further resistance. There he held out for some time against various attacks, but at last, on March 9, was a second time defeated by Wissmann. Though it proved impossible to secure his person, his resistance was now broken. His ammunition and provisions were almost exhausted, so that he no longer showed himself inaccessible to the proposals of peace made him through Sleman bin Nasor. In April he formally submitted to the Commissioner, who forgave him the past, in the hope that his influence over the numerous natives he ruled might in the future further the German cause. Though this hope was not realized in the long-run, it was of great advantage at that critical time to have gained him even as a temporary ally.

The winning back of the north soon followed the reconquest of the south. The towns of Mikindani and Sudi submitted voluntarily, and here again it was Sleman bin Nasor who successfully conducted the negotiations. The services which he rendered to the German cause in those dark days should never be forgotten. The ports of Kilwa and Lindi were occupied early in May, after bombardment from the sea, and received permanent garrisons. A station was also established at Mikindani. The suppression of the rising was thus complete, and at the end of the month Wissmann was able to go home on leave, so as to restore his health, which had been sorely injured by fourteen months' continual exertions.

In the meantime measures had been taken at Berlin to secure international recognition for the African territories just purchased with German blood. As a supplement to the London Convention of November 1, 1886, a new treaty was concluded with England, by which the colonies of German and British East Africa were constituted in their present shape.

Great Britain undertook to exert all her influence to induce the Sultan by friendly means to cede the strip of coast still belonging to him for a reasonable compensation. Germany in return recognised the British protectorate over the possessions retained by the Sultan, including Zanzibar and Pemba, and left to British influence the territory of Witu, to which Germany had acquired certain rights by compacts with its Sultan. The numerous claims renounced by Germany in Africa were compensated by the cession of the island of Heligoland. This British protectorate over the Sultan's territory was proclaimed on November 4, 1890.

As is well known, the compact was generally regarded as a heavy blow to our colonial policy. Above all, those who knew the conditions from their own observation regretted that we had left to the English the island of Zanzibar, which extended in front of our coastline, and the city of the same name. It is no part of this work to criticize the provisions of that treaty, but this one fact should be pointed out-that at this day the port of Zanzibar commands the whole East African coast; that all the larger German firms, with the

German East African Company and the German East African Line at their head, have their principal establishments there. Zanzibar must be of greater consequence to our coast than the island of Bornholm to the shores of the Baltic. This parallel was drawn in the pamphlet in defence of the Anglo-German agreement.

The amount of the compensation that the Sultan was to receive for the cession of the littoral was fixed by an exchange of notes between the German and British Governments at £200,000 in gold, payable in London by the expiration of the year 1890. The sum was raised by the German East African Company, which for this purpose, as well as for the necessary capital expenditure for agricultural purposes, received the privilege of issuing bonds to bearer to the amount of 10,556,000 marks. This was settled in an agreement on November 20, by which the relations between the Government and the Company were regulated. The chief stipulation of this compact was that from the date of payment of the indemnity the Company transferred all its sovereign rights obtained by treaty with the Sultan of Zanzibar to the Empire. The latter in turn undertook for a considerable number of years to pay the Company 600,000 marks annually out of the proceeds of the Customs, and granted it, in addition, a great number of proprietary rights.

In fulfilment of these stipulations, on January 1, 1891, the Empire took over the government of the newly-established colony, to which Freiherr von Soden, hitherto Governor of Cameron, was appointed. On March 22 Wissmann's troops were transformed into Imperial Constabulary, while on July 1 the management of the Customs also passed into the hands of the Colonial Government.

After an orderly state of affairs had thus been established in the coastal districts, the question arose how to extend German influence further into the interior. To follow the various stages of this development lies outside the scope of our work; we will content ourselves with briefly describing how Tippu Tip's native land, Unyanyembe, was incorporated in the German dominions.

We have already mentioned that Emin, after recovering from his serious accident at Bagamoyo, placed his services at the disposal of the Imperial Government. On April 26, 1890, he set out from Bagamoyo with two officers (Langheld and Dr. Stuhlmann), two under-officers, 100 coloured soldiers, and 400 armed carriers, to bring the district about the lakes under German control. The intention was to diverge from Mpapwa north-westward to the Victoria Nyanza, without touching Tabora. This was the express wish of Wissmann, who knew the balance of power between the Arabs there from his own observations, and was afraid that the appearance of Emin's comparatively slender force would evoke unnecessary alarm, and so hinder a better-equipped advance at a more convenient time. Want of carriers, however, and the need of completing his articles of barter, forced the Pasha, contrary to the original plan, to make for the Arab *entrepot*. The hostilities dreaded did not occur; on the contrary, before reaching Tabora Emin received a missive from the Arabs begging him to hoist the German flag in their town.

The victories of Wissmann over the insurgents had naturally not remained unknown here in the interior. Every native knew that the coast had fallen into German hands, and also realized that if he fell out with the masters of that coast all the treasures that he had stored up at a distance would retain little commercial value, and that whoever ventured along the accustomed homeward path in defiance of the new rulers was simply throwing his life away. Those who still wished to ignore these facts had shortly before had their eyes opened by the example of the murderer Mohammed bin Kasum. Thus their own shrewdness bade the Arabs be on good terms with the Germans. It happened very fortunately, moreover, that an influential trader who was devoted to Wissmann, the Beluchi Ismael, had arrived at Tabora shortly before Emin. Thanks very largely to his powers of persuasion, the Arabs of their own accord solicited German protection. The only one who struggled energetically against the new sovereignty was the chief Sike, but even his opposition was at length broken down by the insistence of the Arabs.

On August 1 Emin hoisted the German flag at Tabora. He concluded a convention with the Arabs, in which they expressly acknowledged German rule in Unyanyembe, but were granted the right of choosing a Vali for themselves. They were unanimous in favour of the 'Besar' Sef bin Saad, who afterwards, when a station was established at Tabora, submitted to its jurisdiction, and has filled the post assigned him by the confidence of his fellow-tribesmen to the satisfaction of the Colonial Government up to the present day.*

The new protectors were not long in want of opportunities for armed interference, in favour of their subjects. The marauding Wangoni were once more on the warpath, and had penetrated into the adjoining territory of Urambo. The German commander Freiherr von Bülow, who had joined the expedition from mpapwa with twenty-five men, was sent to meet them, and at first tried to treat with the assailants. When this failed and the Wangoni only advanced in thicker swarms, he appealed to the Pasha for support, which he received in the shape of Lieutenant Langheld with seventy men, and marched against the enemy, with 2,000 Urambo men at his back as well. Four days' fighting (September 9 to 12) ended in the rout of the Wangoni.

The Pasha had meanwhile marched off in the direction of the Victoria Nyanza, and Langheld, when the fight was over, sent his men after him, remaining behind himself to wait for a further expedition sent into the lake region under the Irishman Stokes and Lieutenant Sigl. Freiherr von Bülow remained for the present at Urambo. Here he was visited by Tippu Tip, who had reached the territory of Unyanyembe shortly before the Pasha's departures. The Arabs, among whom Bülow seems to have been considered a particularly stern master, had indeed warned him against this visit, on the principle, 'Never go to your Prince when you are not summoned.' But the missionary who had received him so kindly, Dr. Shaw, known, on account of his lean little figure, by the name of Mzara Mkiuno,* had persuaded him that a man of his importance might venture into the lion's den. And Tippu Tip went, and cannot find words to express his praise of the honourable reception prepared for him by the man to whom even the Vali of Tabora went with trembling. 'We asked each other after our health, and he offered me tea and coffee. When I left I pitched my camp at the watering-place near him. He sent me all sorts of things and seven

---

* Sef has since died.

* A Kinyamwezi expression, meaning 'hunger in the back.'

oxen to make me quite content.'

Our hero is always happy when he can dilate as lengthily as possible on his good relations with Europeans, less in order to proclaim his loyalty than to display the diplomatic penetration with which he, first among his countrymen, recognized the superior power of the Westerners and the value of being on good terms with them.

As Bülow was recalled from his post soon after Tippu Tip's arrival, they decided to travel to the coast together. But when all was prepared for a start, Tippu Tip was attacked by acute dysentery, which stretched him for a long time on a bed of sickness. For four months he hovered between life and death, and it was only through the untiring care of the White Fathers at Kipalapala that he eventually recovered. Scarcely had he recovered than he set out to appear as soon as possible before the English court. On the day after the Pilgrims' Festival of 1308 (end of July, 1891) he left Tabora, though still so weak that he had to be carried on a litter. After two days he was just able to mount a donkey. It is a remarkable fact, worthy of special notice, that this was the first time that he had used any animal for riding; his previous long journeys had all been covered on foot.

At Mpapwa the missionaries told him a strange story of his friend Stanley. He had, it appears, spread the report in Europe that Jameson had bought a girl slave at Yambuya, and in his presence had her killed and devoured by the Manyema. The story naturally evoked general indignation, and Jameson's widow went herself with her brother-in-law to Africa to collect on the spot proofs of the groundlessness of the accusations made against her late husband. While Mrs. Jameson remained behind at Zanzibar, her brother-in-law equipped an expedition to meet Tippu Tip, and question him as to what he knew of the matter. He turned back, however, at Mpapwa, presumably because he was by then fully convinced that the whole horrible story, by which his brother's good name had been endangered, was a malevolent fabrication.

Documentary evidence as to this episode is unhappily not at my disposal, but it is mentioned also by the well-known writer Henryk Sienkiewicz, who was staying at Zanzibar at the same time as Mrs. Jameson, in his 'Letters from Africa' (pp. 114 *et seq.*)-the silliest work, I may remark, that was ever written on African matters. He reports that Jameson had been universally condemned on the strength of Stanley's story, which was believed, and that the position of his widow in the English community was a most painful one.

Tippu Tip was beside himself when he heard of these accusations, and gave vent to his feelings in the following terms: 'The story is a lie. I was not there, but neither saw nor heard anything of it till to-day among you. That he-Jameson-could do such a thing is absolutely impossible. Or do you think that I would tolerate such a thing? But I have never seen a European or any other being that could lie like this fellow. And how can the people judge whether he is lying?'

And he went on furiously soliloquizing: 'All the great kindnesses that I showed him were not enough for him-by way of thanks he wants to drown me now as well. I had a specimen in the promises that he made me: "When I get to Europe I do not know what I shall not give you, for I shall obtain boundless wealth and great influence." And he sent me his photograph! And when we met again he presented me at Cape Town with a dog. I at once passed it on to Jameson. It was a wretched little dog. I knew that he was a liar. No, it was not enough for him to malign me after his cheating. He maligned a dead man-Jameson-as well.'

On the further march through Usagara, Tippu Tip received a letter from the Governor, inviting him to a consultation. He reached the coast at Bagamoyo, and was, as he again proudly mentions, received with high honour by the Head of the District, Schmidt. Then Freiherr von Soden came himself to fetch him to Dar es Salaam, the new capital. After he had stayed there a few days he crossed to Zanzibar.

The period appointed by the court had, of course, long since expired, but of all the threats that had been set forth in its summons none had come to pass. Stanley had failed in his accusations, and his own agent, the representative of Smith, Mackenzie and Co., invited Tippu Tip to his house, where a joint document was signed, by which Tippu Tip and Stanley withdrew their respective demands. The matter was thus finally settled. 'But few Europeans inquired about it, owing to Stanley's lies in the Jameson affair'

CHAPTER XVI

THE COLLAPSE OF THE ARAB POWER

'As if whipped by invisible spirits, the sun-horses of Time break away with the light chariot of our fate, and nothing is left us but bravely and calmly to hold fast the reins, and guide the wheels now right, now left, to avoid here a stone and there an overthrow. Whither the way lies, who knows? He scarcely remembers whence he came.'-GOETHE: *Egmont.*

Since that time Tippu Tip has made no more journeys to the interior; he was spared the spectacle of the complete collapse of the Arab power in the districts he had ruled. As mentioned in the previous chapter, Emin had on August 1 hoisted the German flag at Tabora, and soon after Lieutenant Sigl established a permanent station there. His position was not an easy one, for the Arabs, who at first readily accepted the German domination, had been enraged to the utmost by the news that the Pasha had executed several of their countrymen on the Victoria Nyanza, and through them the chief Sike, who had only submitted unwillingly, was once more encouraged to resistance.

As long as Sigl himself was head of the station peace was at least outwardly preserved. After he was relieved Sike proceeded to open hostilities. On June 6, 1892, an attempt was made by Sigl's successor, Dr. Schwesinger, with the aid of the antislavery expedition under Count Schweinitz, which was there at the time, to storm Quikuru, the chief's *boma*; but it failed, and various subsequent engagements brought no decided success. At length, on January 13, 1893, Lieutenant Prince succeeded, after a fierce fight, in storming Sike's stronghold, when the chief himself and many of his adherents lost their lives by an explosion.

It is worthy of mention that during these conflicts Tippu Tip's stepmother, Nyaso, constantly showed herself well disposed towards the Germans; indeed, she actively supported the last decisive assault by supplying eighty carriers.

Upon Sike's death the German rule in Tabora was permanently established. Sigl, who soon afterwards again took over the control of the station, could now proceed to extend our influence further westward. The road to Lake Tanganyika was by no means secure, and complaints of the plundering of caravans were still constantly coming in; numerous local chiefs were at feud with each other, and so caused disorder in their own and the neighbouring territories. To add to this came the announcement that Mohammed bin Khalfan Rumalisa, the so-called Vali of Ujiji, in the presence of a numerous gathering, had torn up and trampled upon a German flag presented to him by Emin, with threats of war to the knife against the Germans. He was also suspected-with good reason, as it afterwards proved-of having supported the rebel Sike with an armed force shortly before the decisive encounter. His troops, however, were surprised by natives on their entry into Urambo; 200 men were slaughtered, and the rest took to flight.

The Wahehe, too, who on August 17, 1891, treacherously destroyed a strong expedition under von Zalewski, commander of the constabulary, were, according to Tippu Tip's statements, supported by Rumalisa.

In order to take advantage as far as possible of the widespread impression produced by the defeat of Sike, Sigl decided to march at once to Lake Tanganyika in person. He left Tabora on June 19, restored order everywhere on the way, reconciled various Sultans to German rule, and reached Ujiji on July 24. A day's march short of that place the Arabs came to meet him and assure him of their loyalty. He hoisted the German flag at Ujiji, and set up Msabbah bin Nyem el Shehebi as Vali, with the consent of the inhabitants.

Rumalisa had thought it better not to await the arrival of the German leader. True, in numerous letters he had given expression to his unalterable friendship; but he must have had a bad conscience with regard to his former intrigues, for, without informing his fellow-tribesmen, he crossed the lake in a small boat, and, as we shall see later, gave much trouble to the Belgians, whom no less than the Germans he regarded as his natural enemies.

This expedition of Sigl's effectively subdued the German sphere of interest as far as its extreme western frontier. Meanwhile the Belgians had not been idle in making their control a reality in all the districts reserved for them. In the south, during the years 1891-1892, the expeditions of Stairs, Delcommune, and Bia subjugated the territory of Katanga; in order to secure the north and north-east as well, the explorer Van Kerkhove in 1890 made an expedition from Stanley Pool as far as the frontier of Wadelai. On the upper Aruwimi he had many conflicts with slave-stealers, on whom, being provided with excellent military equipment, he inflicted crushing defeats. The tidings of them roused the anger of the Arabs established on the middle Congo, who were all more or less connected with the traders, and felt that the damage done to the latter in their calling must seriously affect themselves. Mwinyi Mohara, the head of the slave-traders at Nyangwe, stirred up a general rising, and at his instigation, in May, 1892, the European Hodister, who lay with a trading expedition on the Congo, south of Stanley Falls, was murdered. The events that resulted from this act of violence, and ended in the total collapse of Arab power to the west of Lake Tanganyika as well, are thus described by Tippu Tip:

'The Belgians, in order to avenge Hodister's death, called on Sef, who, as all knew, represented his father at Stanley Falls, to take arms against Mwinyi Mohara. Sef, who by open hostility towards that influential slave- and ivory-trader would, of course, have alienated all his fellow-tribesmen, replied that he could not venture on such an important step without consulting his father. Then the Belgians broke off the negotiations, and came to terms with Ngongo Luteta.'

This man was, as may be remembered, a slave of Tippu Tip's, and had been placed by his master as his representative in his most especial domain of Utetera, between the Lomami and the Congo. After Tippu Tip's departure from Stanley Falls, he became fairly

COLLAPSE OF THE ARAB POWER

independent, and ventured on various raids into the territory on the left bank of the Lomami. The Belgians, therefore, made war on him, and after he had been several times defeated, in the middle of 1892 he submitted to Commandant Dhanis, who then established a military post in the immediate neighbourhood of his chief town, Ngandu.

Sef-so Tippu Tip declares-knew nothing of the peace between Ngongo Luteta and the Belgians. He was indignant that a vassal of his father's, after committing various other acts outside his prerogative, should have carried on war on his own account. He tried several times to induce Ngongo Luteta to give way, but the latter simply had Sef's messengers knocked on the head. Sef thus found himself compelled to advance in arms against the recalcitrant slave. Then, to his astonishment, the Belgians, towards whom he had no hostile intentions, suddenly intervened on behalf of Ngongo Luteta. He was thus forced into war with them against his will and simply through a misunderstanding.

So Tippu Tip, cautiously as he expresses himself, throws the blame of beginning hostilities on the Belgians, who conspired with his vassal behind his son's back. It is hardly conceivable that Sef, who, as successor to his father at Stanley Falls, was in the closest touch with the Government of the Free State, could have been ignorant of the *rapprochement* between Ngongo Luteta and the Belgians; more especially, the fact that Dhanis had established a station near Ngandu cannot have remained unknown to him, and must have given him matter for reflection. Tippu Tip's account is obviously the outcome of a desire to relieve his son of the responsibility for events which he himself doubtless deeply regretted.

It has often been contended that Tippu Tip as Vali of the Congo State always played a double game, but proofs have not yet been adduced of this imputation. When he accepted the appointment offered him by Stanley, he certainly did so with the intention of rescuing whatever was possible in the districts he had once ruled over. That he could not hold these by force of arms against the Belgians as they pressed forward from the West he had long since convinced himself, knowing as he did the superior resources of the Europeans; nor did the temporary successes which during his absence the Arabs achieved in their struggle with the Belgians lead him astray on that head. He knew that after the loss of their station they would come with a fresh military levy, and recover their lost ground with interest. Thus it remained, as matters stood, the most advantageous plan for the Arabs to live at peace with the Europeans as long as they possibly could. There was business enough still to be done in little frequented regions of boundless extent. There was ivory everywhere in rich abundance, and the new masters could not at one blow sweep away the lucrative slave trade.

It was certainly not an easy position which Tippu Tip occupied as intermediary between the two conflicting elements, but the respect he enjoyed among his countrymen as a member of an old Arab family and the lord of thousands of slaves, the superior astuteness with which he always recognised the right course, and the steadiness of old age, which kept him from imprudences, enabled him to reconcile differences that it seemed impossible to bridge over. Had he not been on the spot for several years as the vassal of the Congo State, the fire that smouldered under the ashes would certainly have burst out sooner. Let us try to realize the situation: On the one side the Arabs, the ancient masters of the country, who for years had carried on a calling which, according to their views, was justifiable; on the other, an intruding European Power, which endeavoured step by step to restrict them in the exercise of what they conceived to be their fairly won rights. The contrasts were too sharp for a lasting peace to be possible.

As soon as Tippu Tip left the scene and his personal influence vanished with him, there was bound sooner or later to be a catastrophe. The Arabs from their standpoint needed no excuse if they at length took arms; nor does any reproach attach to Tippu Tip's youthful son Sef for allowing himself to be induced by the insistence of the Arabs, whose most vital interests were affected, to attack the Belgians. A day of reckoning between Arabs and Europeans in those districts was a historical necessity, which had been postponed through the influence of a great personality, but could not be wholly avoided.

Let us, then, leave it an open question whether Sef desired war with the Belgians or not; in any case, by his attack on Ngongo Luteta hostilities were commenced, and events took the course which they were bound to take. 'It was decreed that the matter should end badly,' says the fatalist autobiographer.

In detail the course of the struggle was as follows:* Sef, for reasons which we will leave undetermined, had attacked Ngongo Luteta. The Belgians, who had received in good time information of the enemy's intentions, came to the rescue of their new vassal, and Sef and his bands, who had pressed forward to the Lomami, after sharp fighting from November, 1892, to January 11, 1893, were driven back to the Congo. Mwinyi Mohara, who had taken part in the campaign, was killed, and a nephew of Tippu Tip's, Sef bin Juma, was drowned in the Lomami.

Dhanis, the leader of the Belgian troops, pursued the Arabs, and encamped opposite Nyangwe, on the left bank of the Congo, on January 29, 1893. The river is at that point 120 yards wide, and he could not cross it, for the Arabs had taken all their boats across with them. He therefore contented himself with bombarding the settlements of the Arabs from his side of the stream. The latter, however, rashly assumed the offensive by crossing the river and establishing two camps opposite the position of the Belgians. They were routed by Dhanis after a day's fighting, and had to flee back to the right bank. By this success the Belgians gained the sympathies of the natives, who now aided them by bringing to the spot the boats necessary for crossing the stream. On March 4 Nyangwe fell, without further fighting, into Dhanis's hands.

At Kassongo the news of the defeat of the Arabs on the Lomami and the death of Mwinyi Mohara evoked great bitterness. It had been erroneously reported that Tippu Tip's son had also fallen. Fugitives had, it appears, reported that his *mtoto* (which means son as well as nephew) Sef had lost his life. The Arabs and natives, who at the name Sef thought first of the son of our hero, were convinced that he was a victim of the conflict, and out of revenge murdered the Europeans living in Kassongo.

After giving his troops a short rest at Nyangwe, Dhanis marched against Kassongo on April 17, and captured it, with the help of Ngongo Luteta, on the 22nd of that

---

* *Cf.*, **for the sketch that follows, the periodical** *Le Mouvement Géographique* **for February 4, 1884.**

COLLAPSE OF THE ARAB POWER

month, after furious fighting. In wild flight the Arabs abandoned the field, and many of them were drowned in the River Musokoi. A great booty fell into the hands of the victors, amongst other things 3 tons of ivory, 20 hundred-weight of powder, and as many repeating rifles. A lucky find was made here, too, in the discovery of the last leaves of the diary of Emin Pasha, who had been murdered meanwhile.

While the Arabs were thus harried in the southern districts, in the north also Lieutenant Chaltin had conducted an expedition against the insurgents from Basoko, the junction of the Lomami and the Congo. He had steamed up the Congo and the Lomami, had there taken possession, without a blow, of the settlements of Yangi, Bena, Kamba, and Lomo, which the Arabs had abandoned, and finally, on April 22, marched overland to the Arab station of Riba Riba, on the left bank of the Congo, which he also found deserted. He rightly reflected that the fugitive Arabs must have retired to their headquarters at Stanley Falls, and from Bena Kamba he proceeded there on board the steamer *Ville de Bruxelles*, which was at his disposal. On the way, near the mouth of the Lomami, a letter reached him from Tobbak, the Commandant of Stanley Falls, which showed that his surmise was quite correct.

The Arabs there had received intelligence of the defeats of their compatriots at Nyangwe and Kassongo, and were now gathering all their available fighting strength to strike a decisive blow at the Europeans. After various minor skirmishes, the Dutch factory was attacked during the night of May 11. Next day the settlement of the Belgian Upper Congo Company was occupied by the Shensis in the service of the Arabs, two Government boats were fired on, and an attack on the station itself attempted.

Tobbak was holding out with difficulty against superior numbers, when on the 18th, at the moment of his greatest extremity, the *Ville de Bruxelles* drew near with the longed-for relief force under Chaltin. On its appearance the Arabs took to flight, and the town remained in the hands of the Europeans. About the middle of July Commandant Ponthier, who had returned from leave in Europe, took the station of Kirundu, above Stanley Falls. The insurgents suffered a severe defeat: twenty-eight chiefs were taken prisoner and 1,000 rifles fell into the hands of the victors.

Thus the power of the Arabs on the Congo was shattered. Such of them as escaped retreated to Lake Tanganyika, and there joined the forces of Rumalisa, who meanwhile had resumed his baffled plan of attacking the Belgians westward of the lake. As he had some 3,000 rifles at his disposal, he was able for some time to press hard on Captain Jacques, who was in those parts. But the latter summoned reinforcements, and with the help of two officers, Delcommune and Joubert, succeeded, in September, 1892, in driving the Arab partisans back on Albertville.

When the fugitives from Kassongo arrived, Rumalisa once more marshalled a strong army, and marched with it to meet the advancing Belgians under Dhanis and Ponthier. On October 20, 1893, a sanguinary engagement took place on the river Luama, ending, after heavy losses on both sides, in a decisive victory for the Europeans. The Belgians lost their commander Ponthier, who a few days later succumbed to wounds received in the action. Tippu Tip's son Sef also, with numerous other Arabs, paid for the attack with his life.

This blow broke the power of the Arabs westward of Lake Tanganyika as well, and such of the survivors as did not fall into the hands of the victors took their way through German territory back to their homes, and since then have never attempted open resistance to the European power.

In truth in the time that followed this would have been scarcely possible. On July 2, 1890, the Anti-slavery Conference at Brussels had adopted its well-known General Declaration, which, in the endeavour to cope with the ravages of the African slave trade, contained strict regulations as to the trade in fire-arms and ammunition as well. The Belgians, who previously used to sell Tippu Tip and his people powder in unlimited quantities, now, after the woeful experiences that they had had in the matter, of course stood out for the exact observance of these regulations.

Tippu Tip was kept *au courant* of all the warlike events in his former province by his adherents, but we may implicitly believe his assurance that he had no share in the even, on the contrary regretted them. All letters that came in he laid before the German and British Consuls for their information. Through their reports, by the round-about way of Zanzibar, many occurrences were known in Europe before they became officially public via Brussels.

Our hero saw plainly that he could no longer check the course of events, and bore the many losses which befell him personally with the stoical calm of the Moslem. The war had cost him 4,500 *frasilas* of ivory, 700 loads of fabric for garments, and 20,000 muskets. He could, however, console himself with the treasures which he had gradually placed in safety. Numerous *shambas* and houses in Zanzibar and on the coast were his property.

But even these were now for the most part to be subject to dispute. Rumalisa, who escaped with his life from the disastrous fights on Lake Tanganyika, had fled by secret ways (for he dreaded the vengeance of the Germans) to the coast, and had been taken across to Zanzibar in a fishing-boat; he now came forward suddenly with a claim to the effect that Tippu Tip owed him a quarter of his fortune. He produced a document setting forth that he, Tippu Tip, and Bwana Nzige had formed a partnership, by which all profits that they might earn were to be divided between them; Tippu Tip was to receive a half, the other two a quarter apiece.

Our hero has always disputed the authenticity of this document, as did his cousin Bwana Nzige. They both declared that their signatures appended to it were forgeries. The result was a lengthy lawsuit before the court at Dar es Salaam, which Rumalisa won. This decision gave rise to a long contest as to the amount of the quarter to be handed over by Tippu Tip, ending in a judicial settlement by which Tippu Tip gave up his whole property on the coast to his opponent, the particular items being specified in an inventory.

It soon proved, however, that various objects of value transferred by him did not exist, amongst others a quantity of ivory supposed to be buried at Itahua, and a claim for a debt of 6,000 dollars. As Tippu Tip, who is a Zanzibari subject, was no longer liable, after the surrender of his property on the coast, to be sued in the German colony, Rumalisa raised a claim in the Sultan's court for compensation for the valuables not forthcoming. According to the principles obtaining, he was recognised as a German subject, and his plaint was supported by the German Consulate, which took advantage of its treaty rights to have the sittings of the court watched by a representative, and the present writer, to whom this duty was allotted, was thus for the first time enabled to make the acquaintance of the hero of this story, to be sure in somewhat unfriendly manner. After a protracted litigation it was at last declared in the court of appeal by the Sultan himself that the defendant, in fulfilment of the settlement, must pay a further sum of 6,000 dollars.

The plaintiff, it must be admitted, was not much the gainer thereby. The sum adjudged him was for the most part swallowed up by the lawyer's fees, and so many creditors were lying in wait for the remainder that soon after his success he announced his bankruptcy, which is still pending before the district court of Dar es Salaam. Tippu Tip consoled himself with the thought that the old proverbs 'Mali ya haramu yanakwenda nyia ya haramu' Ill-gotten gains never prosper-had once more been verified.

Yet another lawsuit gave the Sheikh a great deal of trouble. The heirs of his business friend Taria Topan, who had died towards the end of the eighties, declared that at the time of his death Tippu Tip still owed him 15,000 rupees, and brought an action for this sum. The examination of the books ordered by the court showed that, on the contrary, our hero had still 35,000 rupees to receive from his banker. He now 'turned the spear the other way,' and claimed of Taria's grandson, Saleh, who had taken over the business later on, not only the payment of this amount, but of a further considerable sum which was due to him from their later business connections. As a result he not long since obtained a valid judgment for the not inconsiderable amount of 300,000 rupees; but he will not set eyes on much of this money, for Saleh has long since run through his inheritance from his grandfather.

On the other hand, all this litigation has entailed heavy sacrifices on our hero. The English lawyer who acted for him pocketed the magnificent fee of 20,000 rupees (about £1,350) for his pains.

Tippu Tip has not again come to the fore politically since his final return to Zanzibar, but, as in his earlier years, he has always tried to be on good terms with the rulers for the time being. Seyyid Ali, who was ruling on his arrival, had long been his personal friend, and always treated him with goodwill, even though, as Tippu Tip complains, he was avaricious and not over-free with presents to his favourites. Hamed bin Thweni, who succeeded him, was ill-disposed to Tippu Tip, because he had once outbid him at the purchase of a *shamba* on which the Prince had cast his eye. Not till shortly before Hamed's death were the relations between them improved.

It is well known that when this Sultan died, Seyyid Bargash's youthful son Khalid endeavoured to ascend the throne, contrary to the wish of the protecting Power. He garrisoned the palace, and a whole English squadron was needed to drive him out of it. When further resistance proved impossible the young Prince fled from the building, which was collapsing over his head, to the German Consulate, and, after finding refuge there for a month, was conveyed across to Dar es Salaam in a German man-of-war, where he now lives as the guest of the Empire, and dreams of his past splendour as Sultan.

Tippu Tip was on terms of most cordial friendship with the energetic and warmhearted son of his former patron, and honestly strove to restrain him from the folly of bidding defiance with his handful of warriors to a great European Power. In the certainty that such resistance would be unsuccessful, he kept aloof from the struggle, which brought financial ruin on many highly-placed Arabs, whose participation in it was visited by heavy fines.

His cousin Hamud bin Mohammed was appointed Hamed's successor. He formed a close friendship with Tippu Tip, and always reckoned him one of his confidential advisers. On two journeys which he made to the African mainland the Sheikh was among his few companions.

Since Hamud's death, which took place in 1904, his son Ali, a minor, has been reigning; but he is under the guardianship of the English Premier, and as yet has little say in the affairs of government. As he was brought up in English fashion, he is but little in touch with Arab circles.

Tippu Tip is, nevertheless, still an important personage in the Council of Zanzibar, and where it is a question of doing something for the country he is one of the first to be asked his views. In his mockingly superior way he is accustomed on such occasions to be not at all backward with his opinion.

He knows, however, that the times of Arab glory are past, and possesses no further political ambition. With the youthful activity which he has preserved even into his old age, this man of nearly seventy attends untiringly to his numerous personal affairs. His fortune still amounts to £50,000 in round figures, and is very advantageously invested in stone houses and landed property.

His longing is some day to behold the magic land of Europe, of whose splendour he had a foretaste at Cape Town. A pilgrimage is also still expected of him by Allah, for the Koran lays down that every Moslem whose means admit of it should at least once in his life undertake the journey to the holy city of Mecca.

His idea is to combine the two journeys, and as in his robust old age he still counts on many more years of life, he hopes to be able, sooner or later, to carry out the plan. 'In sha Allah!'

Tippu Tip died at Zanzibar, of malaria, on June 13, 1905. The death of Wissmann followed on the very next day; that of Stanley had taken place a year earlier. Thus within a brief period of time three of the most striking personalities among those who wrested its secrets from the Dark Continent have passed away.

Dwellers at a distance may find something strange in this juxtaposition of the slave-hunter's name with those of the two world-famed explorers; to one who has followed the destinies of our hero it will be intelligible enough. Tippu Tip was no dainty draughtsman, yet the paths traced out by his blood-stained hand have supplied the framework for all the subsequent cartography of German East Africa and the Congo Free State. Thus a life-work of destruction has served to aid the advance of civilization.